ACT OF ONE

ACT OF ONE

Foreword by Andrew Chaikin, Author of *A Man on the Moon*

Victoria Barna and Bruce A. Tully

EVOLVING JOURNEYS
PUBLISHING HOUSE

DEDICATION

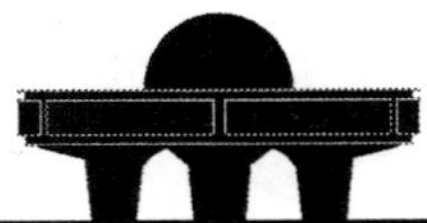

This book is dedicated to Dr. Joseph Tugligowitz, Bruce A. Tully's grandfather who inspired Bruce and served as a role model. He was bigger than life! Not only a community leader, Dr. Tugligowitz was an aristocratic Baron but still humble as well as noble, compassionate, kind and generous. During his lifetime he was known as the man who could get the job done, and he was loved by everyone.

Grandfather, father, husband, friend, doctor and teacher were only a few of his roles. He lived a life of service. Even when he knew he was dying he regretted that he hadn't done more.

We are grateful for the exemplary life that he led as he showed us how to live a life of service every day.

DEDICATION V

ACKNOWLEDGEMENTS

I want to thank my wife, Jeanne, and son, Joel, who inspire me.

Jeanne, your unconditional dedication, commitment, love, faith and trust in me have made my life and this project easier.

Joel, you inspire me daily. You persevere, work hard and accomplish your goals. You never waiver. I am honored and proud to be your Dad.

Robert Yowell, you're the catalyst for writing *ACT OF ONE*. Without your due diligence and interest in my story as well as your subsequent article that was published in the *Smithsonian Magazine*, we would not have this book.

Dr. Ward A. Shoemaker, you gave me the "green light" to pursue my mission when teachers and administrators were ready to suspend me from school and destroy my work. Thank you. Without you, I wouldn't have a story.

Dr. Monroe E. Spaght of Shell Oil US, you listened and opened the door to the next step.

Theodore J. Kauffeld, you served as sponsor, mentor and guide as I transitioned and transformed from a carefree, joking jock to a serious man.

~Bruce A. Tully

ACKNOWLEDGEMENTS

I would like to thank Bruce A. Tully for trusting me with his story and having confidence in me to tell it.

Thank you to my husband, Robert, for supporting me throughout the process of writing this story. You inspire me, and you believed in me long before I believed in myself. Your unconditional love and support were steadfast as you read the story as it developed. Thank you for your helpful insights and suggestions to provide clarity for the reader.

Thank you to my sons, Tim and Nick. You inspire me as I watch the men you have become and the values and integrity that you live by. You cheered me on and encouraged me to keep going. Your enthusiasm for this story was contagious.

~Victoria Barna

ACKNOWLEDGEMENTS IX

FOREWORD

Until I met Bruce Tully I thought I knew what it meant to be a Cold War Warrior at the dawn of the Space Age. I had interviewed the astronauts and flight controllers from NASA's pioneering early missions as well as written about that electrifying era when the heavens became the new arena of the Cold War, the battle of ideologies between the United States and the Soviet Union. When I thought of America's Space Age Cold War Warriors, I pictured astronauts in silvery spacesuits—or maybe the pocket-protected engineers at their consoles in mission control. Then I heard Bruce tell his story, the story you now hold in your hands. It's the story of a young man fighting his own personal Cold War.

In the late 1950s Bruce was a typical American teenager with football and girls on his mind. His greatest battles were fought on the gridiron. All that changed on a September day in 1959 when he and his high school classmates took a trip to the United Nations, where they heard Soviet Premier Nikita Khrushchev address the General Assembly. Hearing

Khrushchev dismiss American youth as weak and lazy, Tully was so infuriated that he vowed to prove him wrong. Fired by the anti-Communist passions of his beloved Russian grandfather, the man he later called his mentor, Tully conceived of the Astronarium—a combination of "astronautics" and "planetarium"—as a kind of temple to America's achievements in space, for the upcoming New York World's Fair. Making the Astronarium a reality became Tully's obsession.

To carry out his plan, Tully would have to transform himself from a varsity jock into a science nerd. In other words, he would need to discover a different kind of strength. And, in the process he would have to fight an even more personal battle with his own father, who dismissed his dream with, "Who do you think is going to listen to you? You're just a stupid kid from New Jersey!" As you will see, the answer to that question turned out to exceed the young man's wildest dreams.

As you accompany Bruce Tully on this extraordinary adventure, you will journey with him into America's corridors of power as he meets some of the country's most important men, from the president of Shell Oil to the new U.S. President John F. Kennedy. Tully's once-in-a-lifetime encounters continue as he travels to Cape Canaveral where he meets with the "Original Seven" Mercury astronauts, who are preparing for their voyages into space. And on the morning of May 5, 1961, when a Redstone rocket launches Alan Shepard on America's first space flight, Bruce Tully is there to witness the event, and his dreams of the Astronarium and Science Center seem to soar skyward right along with it.

Let Bruce Tully take you back to a time when America's greatness was tested by a bold reach into the heavens. The power of this story lies in witnessing Tully's own transformation from the teenager sitting in the visitors' gallery of the United Nations wearing jeans and a varsity jacket into the young man in a Brooks Brothers' suit addressing Congress. It's a journey that will resonate with anyone, young or old, who has faced—or may now be facing—the challenges of making his or her most cherished dreams come true.

~Andrew Chaikin, author of *A Man on the Moon*

TABLE OF CONTENTS

Dedication v

Acknowledgements – Bruce A. Tully vii

Acknowledgements – Victoria Barna ix

Foreword – Andrew Chaikin xi

Table of Contents xv

Prologue 1

How It Began..5

The Mission Evolves..11

Leading by Example...13

A Personal Challenge Is Declared 23

A Defining Moment 31

A Blessing in Disguise 35

Against All Odds 45

The *Manifesto* Is Created 55

The Vision and the Mission Take Form 61

Choices, Consequences and Rewards 67

The Moment of Truth 75

Welcome to New York City 81

Knocking on Doors..91

Perseverance Pays Off 97

Next Step – The Engineers......109

A Job Offer 121

Can We Build It? 131

Back to Basics......139

Sharing the Astronarium Story 151

Enter the Architects 155

Bedlam!......161

A Professional Passion Is Discovered 165

We Are Ready! 169

Back to Work 173

A Short Break......177

Traveling in Style 179

Department of Commerce Committee Presentation 183

Appearing on the *Today Show* 187

Coast to Coast 191

A Standing Ovation 195

A New President Brings Hope 197

Lunch at the White House......201

A Gauntlet Is Tossed 211

A Promise Kept 217

Cape Canaveral and the Astronauts 223

Momentum Builds 229

Making History 231

It's a Go! 237

A Congressional Committee Invitation......241

A Surprising and Unexpected Invitation 243

Youth Are Our Future 245

Amazing Decisions and Trips 251

Victoria's Epilogue 253

Bruce's Epilogue 257

Introduction to Appendix I – Robert Yowell....................261

Appendix I 263

Introduction to Appendix II – Victoria 271

Appendix II 273

PROLOGUE

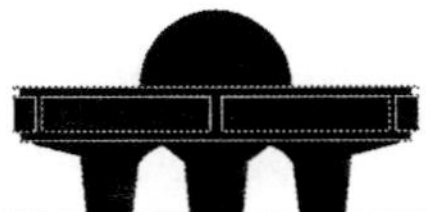

Warriors are ageless and timeless and they have appeared throughout history. Some are well known and others are not. Here is a story that many of you may not believe. It took place fifty years ago and our warrior is a sixteen-year-old high school student named Bruce A. Tully.

Bruce grew up *tough* in an urban working class family. He grew up in what some people called the "blue collar ghettos," one of the ethnic neighborhoods of New Jersey. Oil refineries and chemical plants surrounded the neighborhood. Smoke stacks billowed across the meadowlands.

Where he lived didn't matter. Who people thought he was didn't matter. At sixteen years of age he knew these opinions really didn't matter. He had strong convictions and refused to let anything stop him from trying to accomplish the impossible. He had the heart of a warrior. He began to fulfill his mission against all odds.

Some people called him a hero. His teachers didn't understand him or his passion to persevere and school administrators threatened him with suspension from school.

His parents had little time to offer their support. His mother had her hands full. She worked and took care of his brother and sister who were both under the age of six. She fondly thought of Bruce as a dreamer and didn't want him to be hurt. His father traveled for his job and was frequently away from home; however, in the beginning as Bruce's mission began to unfold he felt that Bruce was wasting his time. In the end his father came around and fully supported him as he became personally involved.

In spite of significant obstacles along the way Bruce chose to keep moving forward and remain focused on his mission. He was courageous and he persevered. Turning points were encountered, like forks in the road, moments that presented choices where he could keep going or stop, where he could remain honest or lie for his supposed advantage.

Bruce chose to keep going and maintain his integrity. What he accomplished was amazing. He is an example of how one person can bring an idea into form without having a clue as to how to make it happen, of how a mission can be made real against all odds!

Throughout his quest Bruce persevered and he gathered strength as he believed in himself and his vision. In spite of the obstacles he encountered he worked hard and found support that came from many powerful people including industry leaders, Fortune 500 CEOs, national news reporters, astronauts and the President of the United States. Imagine what it took for a sixteen-year-old boy to have these powerful allies who offered their encouragement and help.

This young warrior and his experiences are examples of what is possible. One person can make a difference. He shows us that commitment and focus on a mission takes courage, vision and is transforming.

Following Bruce on his journey will show you how he came to understand his purpose and how he learned to trust what he believed to be true. He demonstrated how anyone can be a warrior. You don't have to be a fantasy character or super hero to accomplish what appears to be impossible. Anyone can fight for what he or she believes regardless of age.

All it takes is an *Act of One!*

Join us now on Bruce's amazing and miraculous journey!

PROLOGUE 3

HOW IT BEGAN

Nothing was more important to Bruce than his family. His family background and history created the foundation and direction his life would take. His family and, more specifically, his Grandpa Joseph influenced what he believed in, his values, perceptions and his purpose in life.

He was born into a family of warriors that started with his great-great-great-grandfather who led an army of Cossack warriors to defeat Napoleon and his army. They were independent, unconventional and fiercely loyal men. Because of this unprecedented win against Napoleon and his ancestor's loyalty, the ruling Czar of Russia rewarded his family for their great service. An aristocratic title of Baron was bestowed upon his great-great-great-grandfather along with land that took twenty days and twenty nights to cover riding on horseback in what was known as the Bread Basket of Russia, the Ukraine.

Moving forward several generations, as this aristocratic family prospered and during the time of Bruce's grandfather, political unrest developed once again. With the help of their serfs and servants, at great risk to themselves and all that they held dear, Bruce's grandparents were smuggled out of Russia. In grave danger they found their way from Russia to the United States to escape the Russian Revolution and the brutality of the Communist regime. They left with only the clothes on their backs.

It took great courage, faith and trust to escape Russia and move a family to an unknown country with nothing, leaving everything they had behind. This strong family legacy is what helped form Bruce into who he would become.

As his grandparents arrived at Ellis Island, the immigration entry point to the United States on the East Coast, the officers quickly Anglicized their Russian surname. Tugligowitz became Tully. So, they began with nothing. They were no longer known by their own family name. They really started over.

As a young boy Bruce was very close to his grandfather, a Russian Orthodox priest, physician, fervent anti-Communist Czarist aristocrat, Russian Baron and Cossack tribal leader. He grew up listening to his Grandpa Joseph's stories and teachings until he passed away. Bruce loved his grandfather and thought he was an extraordinary man.

As Bruce grew older he remembered the time he spent with his Grandpa Joseph and he recognized how much he was influenced by his beliefs, values and practices. He believed that his grandfather was a living example of all that was good. He was someone who dedicated his life to help those who were less fortunate than himself.

Bruce remembered seeing him always in his three-piece suit. He remembered how his Grandpa Joseph always carried himself with an air of nobility and dignity. He demonstrated daily through his actions what was possible and always practiced what he preached. Bruce thought of him as a living example of how someone overcomes hardship and rises to the top.

He remembered how his grandparents arrived in the United States with nothing but the clothes on their backs. Eventually his grandfather, Dr. Tully, created five medical clinics that provided medical care to Eastern European immigrants while helping to clothe and feed the poor as well.

His Grandpa Joseph's deep values of compassion, courage and caring for others were embedded in Bruce and formed a solid foundation for how he would live his life.

Bruce remembered visiting his grandfather's office over the neighborhood grocer's store on Saturdays in Newark, New Jersey. Springfield Avenue, where it was located, was like a mini-European melting pot that teemed with life. Everyone was friendly and greeted each other in their own languages. People lined up outside the building where his Grandpa Joseph's office was located beginning early in the morning. Oftentimes so many people were there and the line was so long that it curled around the building. People knew they would be seen and greeted by Dr. Tully in their own language no matter how long it took.

Dr. Tully treated each person with respect and if they couldn't afford to pay for the visit, he saw them anyway.

Neighborhood mothers came to him when they needed clothing and food for their children. He always sent them to the neighborhood tailor or grocer to take care of their family needs and said, "Tell them to put it on my bill!"

Before seeing patients in his clinic Bruce joined his Grandpa Joseph in his private chapel for prayer. Dr. Tully had created a sacred chapel that included beautiful Russian icons, candles, large wooden furniture and a roaring fireplace. Being an Orthodox priest the chapel and time spent in prayer helped him center, offer gratitude for the many blessings in his life and pray for guidance and support as he treated the patients each day.

Although Bruce was too young to realize it then, as he grew older he began to understand a power was there and something greater. He realized that his grandfather's faith in God was the foundation of his life.

Saturdays spent with Grandpa Joseph were special for Bruce because he knew that when they took a break for lunch they would go to the Jewish deli across the street and have crème soda and a corned beef sandwich.

He remembered other times he spent with his grandfather as well. He listened to stories in the Turkish steam baths where they sat in the steam room with towels over their heads. He also remembered sitting in his lap in a huge, carved wooden chair while his grandfather told him stories.

Bruce came from a large family. His grandparents had twelve sons and on holidays the entire family and their families gathered together to make food baskets for families in the Eastern European ghettos. They delivered them on the doorsteps knowing they would be well received.

Dr. Tully was larger than life to Bruce. He was revered by all who knew him. He was like a shepherd who took care of his flock and had a great extended family. Dr. Tully's extraordinary life and example formed the foundation for the person Bruce would become. Through him he learned to stand up to, face, and combat the forces of evil—evil that threatened to destroy all he believed in and stood for in the world.

This part of Bruce's life story begins during the 1950s at the height of the Cold War between Russia and the United States. During this era many people believed that anything Russian was to be mistrusted, feared and shunned. This was especially true for Bruce.

Bruce believed no evil was greater than the Soviet Union. The seed of distrust was planted as he listened as a young boy to his grandfather's stories. The distrust of the Soviets became stronger as he grew older. Never far from his thoughts was his Grandpa Joseph's warning: "Always be on guard against the evils of Communism. This is what murdered and destroyed our family. Be prepared to fight the Communists at all costs." Bruce was raised to stand up to bullies, regardless of their sizes, and to protect the weak.

When his grandfather became ill Bruce sat at his grandfather's bedside. As Grandpa Joseph lay dying Bruce promised, "I'll continue the fight, the fight to combat evil!"

In that moment, at a very young age, Bruce began to awaken as a visionary. His vision and first mission didn't become clear until several years later when a series of events happened that brought his mission into focus.

THE MISSION EVOLVES

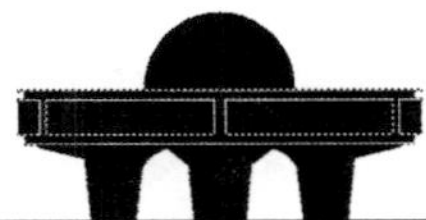

The year is 1959 and Bruce is a sixteen-year-old high school student, a respected and tough jock. Three events took place during high school that identified and clarified what Bruce thought of as his vision and his mission. Two of these events took place on the football field and the other occurred during a Civics Class field trip to the United Nations in New York City.

He wasn't fully aware of it at the time but being an athlete and a tough jock presented many opportunities to test what he believed. He had opportunities to examine his courage and his convictions, and he could make choices to move forward or quit. These experiences laid the groundwork and advanced his mission.

He was sixteen, six foot four inches tall and he weighed one hundred eighty-five pounds. People thought he was older than he was. Sometimes this helped. He was a formidable opponent and often used his physical size to his advantage, especially on the football field or in the boxing ring while he focused on intimidating his opponents. He was mentally tough and a strong leader on and off the field.

LEADING BY EXAMPLE

It was a cold, dark and wet September day in New Jersey. Bruce and the Madison High School football team were in the locker room preparing for a big game with Montclair High, archrival and reigning State champions. Wet, warm steam was floating from some of the showers throughout the locker room. It looked like a castle keep before a battle. Quarters were cramped and you could hear nervous laughter from some of the players. A lot of bumping into each other was going on and some towel snapping too.

The locker room ritual seemed to be an adolescent sacred rite of passage for these high school football players. It had a tribal feel about it where young warriors can go to bond and feel a unity, almost spiritual in nature. It was the way to get ready for battle. Each player entered the locker room feeling "happy go lucky" and they left transformed, like a beast that's battle-ready!

Everyone was amped with adrenalin but they were quiet and solemn as they suited up, putting on their game faces.

They knew it was time to focus. At that moment nothing was more important than this game!

With their game faces on, completely transformed, each player left the locker room and ran out to get on the bus. They stood in the rain and waited their turns to board. Their moods were serious. They were mentally ready and tough and they were thinking about nothing but winning the game. No one dared to laugh or crack a joke. Emotions were high and the air was thick with tension. You could cut the tension with a knife! In the background one of the players said, "Hurry up and get on."

Another player grumbled, "Why do we have to travel in this awful weather? Why couldn't we play here?"

The game strategy was reviewed in the locker room by the Coach and, although some grumbling was going on, you could feel an intensity and excitement radiating from each player. Winning this game was crucial as far as they were concerned. "Winning is important and winning against the reigning New Jersey State champions, Montclair High School, is even better," Bruce thought to himself.

As his teammates talked quietly among themselves on the ride to Montclair High he stared out the window. All he could see were gray skies and rain. Focused and intense as the rain hit the windows of the bus he wondered, "Why can't we catch a break?"

The noise and conversations of his teammates began to penetrate his thoughts. He smelled their fear. Although the players around him talked quietly among themselves, he overheard some talk about losing to the State champions. "I can't believe it. This isn't the attitude to take into this game!" he thought to himself. "It sounds as though we've already lost the game!"

Finally he couldn't stand it so he sarcastically asked, "Hey, why are we even going? Why even bother? You sound as if we have already lost. What are you guys, a bunch of losers? We can play these guys. Don't let Coach hear you talking like this."

As they pulled into the wet and muddy parking lot, Bruce and his teammates checked things out looking through the windows of the bus. The first thing they saw was an intimidating stadium. "Wow, we play on an open grass field with bleachers," he heard one of the players say. "You've got to be kidding."

Bruce saw that the stadium lights were already on. It was getting dark and a cold, rainy mist was swirling through the beams of the lights. The field had an otherworldly feeling. "How are we going to play football in this?" he wondered.

As they began to leave the bus and head for the field they could see the Montclair team showing their strength and size. Montclair players lined up shoulder to shoulder, goal line to goal line. Bruce and his teammates couldn't believe it. It seemed surreal, magical and eerie at the same time. "What's next? Is there a dragon ready to land in the middle of the field?" Bruce mused.

Although a predictable tactic, Montclair High's greeting still made too much of an impression. Madison's team was outnumbered. Only twenty-four players were on the traveling team and they faced what seemed to be at least one hundred Montclair players. Bruce heaved in a deep breath and exclaimed to himself, "We can't let this psych us out!"

Sizing up the Montclair team when warm-ups began on the field the Coach pulled Bruce aside and blurted out, "I need you to play both ways today, defense and offense. This is going to be a tough one. I need you out there."

Bruce knew what he had to do and nodded knowingly. "I'm there for you, Coach."

The team entered the huddle and before the kickoff Bruce took charge. He turned his head and glanced at the Montclair sideline and said, "Hey guys, they put their pads on the same as we do. I don't care how many players they have over there. We didn't come here to lose. Let's get this done!"

Cheering and screaming they left the huddle and the Madison High players rallied and focused on winning the game. Everyone was ready to begin one of the toughest "Jersey style" games they had ever played. The players were tough and hard-hitting and a lot of trash-talking flashed through the air. Madison High was determined and they played like fierce warriors. Bruce played his heart out doing exactly what the Coach asked of him—playing both ways— scoring an essential touchdown and gaining badly needed yardage at critical times.

The State champs were surprised at how fierce and tough Madison High's team played. By half-time the score was tied, 14 to 14. No one thought about the rain and cold anymore. The only thing that was important was winning the game.

The second half began and the game became more physical. As it progressed into the fourth quarter Montclair took a three-point lead. They had the ball on Madison's eighteen-yard line. It was first and ten. Emotions were high. The players were so focused and intense that you could feel the tension on both sides of the field.

Montclair's team was tough. They played like warrior beasts dedicated to protecting their all-star quarterback. He dropped back to pass and was surprised to see Bruce fighting through the last of the defensive line with great effort, skill and perseverance. Bruce realized he had a clear shot at the quarterback. His arm came down with a clean shot and smashed the quarterback's face guard. They both went down! Blitzed!

The sack resulted in a ten-yard loss! Montclair's quarterback was dazed and slow in getting up. Bruce realized that he was injured on the play. In shock he began to feel a lot of pain. He looked down and realized that his arm was bleeding heavily. Bruce yelled, "I think my arm is broken!" As he watched his arm a lump the size of an egg began to grow larger. Madison called its last time-out.

Seeing Bruce down and hurt his good buddy, Charlie, a large black kid, ran over: "Hey, man, are you okay?"

"I think it's broken, man!" groaned Bruce in a lot of pain.

Still on the field a wet, cold and muddy Bruce stayed down on his knees holding his arm. Everyone could tell he was badly hurt. The question everyone was asking was, "Will he continue to play?"

The team trainers finally got to Bruce out on the field. They looked at Bruce's injured arm and one of the trainers said, "It's not broken. It's just a bad bruise."

In pain and exhausted Bruce was soaked to the skin, cold, covered in mud and seriously injured. He looked at the Coach for guidance. "I need a break and I want to come out," he thought to himself. "I've played three and a half quarters of the toughest football of my life. I'm seriously hurt and I'm done."

Coach was someone that Bruce looked up to and admired. He thought the Coach would pull him out because of his injury. The Coach looked away, turned his back and walked away. Bruce suddenly felt all alone. He realized the Coach wasn't going to help him. Several ideas went through his mind all at once. "What is this guy doing? He's not taking me out. What is wrong with him? I'm hurt. Can't I even come out for one play? Fine, I get it. It's all up to me."

The Coach's response to his injury was a major turning point for Bruce. He realized, "Man, this is how life is. I can move forward or quit. Who can I depend on? My Coach just turned his back on me and walked away. Forget him. I'm not playing for him. I'm playing for the guys on the field next to me."

Feeling let down, exhausted and in pain, he had to make a choice. Madison was down three points with less than five minutes left on the game clock. With so many thoughts racing through his head, all he could think about was, "What's the right thing to do? Even though I'm hurt, shall I play through the pain or let the team down? I don't even know how badly I'm hurt. My arm feels as if it's broken. There's no time to come out, hurt or not!"

With a pounding head and a battered body Bruce made up his mind and knew what he needed to do. He didn't want to let the team down. So, he decided to keep playing whether he was hurt or not. "I'll deal with my injured arm after the game is over," he told himself.

Pushing the pain aside, he rejoined the huddle and screamed at his teammates, "We've got to hold them here and we've got to hold them now!"

Charlie yelled, "Let's kill these guys!"

The Madison players were on a mission, a mission to win! It was Montclair's ball, second down and twenty, on the twenty-eighth yard line. Montclair ran a fullback draw for a fourteen-yard gain. The game was on the line. It was third and six and the ball was on the fourteen-yard line.

In Madison's defensive huddle, breathing hard, Bruce predicted, "They're going to fake it up the middle and then pitch it wide to their All-State running back."

Charlie agreed: "Hey, man, they are coming at you! They think you have a bum arm."

"Yeah, I know!" responded Bruce. "Let's do this!"

The game clock was ticking and they had no remaining time-outs. On the next play Montclair ran a sweep. This was a huge play, the play for the win, a game-changing play. Both offensive guards pulled. Then Charlie leveled one of the guards on a penetration block. The remaining offensive line focused on taking Bruce down.

Although injured he played tough as he fought through seven guys on the field and finally was one on one with Montclair's running back. Their eyes locked and after trying to hurdle over Bruce, Bruce tackled him for a loss of yardage! Madison made a huge defensive stand but time was running out. It was Montclair's last down and they lined up for a field goal in the rain. They missed! The unthinkable had happened!

Madison had the ball and the goal line was eighty-four yards away. They were in position to drive for the winning touchdown with three minutes left in the game. Montclair called for their last time-out. The players were impatient.

Defeat was not an option for Bruce and his team. Victory was possible! With the goal line eighty-four yards away Bruce was back in the offensive huddle. He said, "These guys never thought we would be here, NEVER! We can beat these guys. We can beat them."

His mission was clear. Once again he rallied his team. He was their leader and he kept the players focused. Leaving the huddle Charlie screamed, "Let's bring it! Let's put it to 'em!"

The score was close. Only three points separated the winner from the loser. For the next three minutes Madison made a serious drive but had no remaining time-outs! They got within nine yards of the goal line and the clock kept ticking. All of a sudden time ran out!

Victory was snatched away from Madison High on this cold, wet and dreary September day. The team couldn't believe it. Victory was so close and yet so far away. You could hear the loud wail of the victory siren as Montclair ran off the field. They were grateful for the win. The State champions never expected such tough play from Madison High, a bunch of blue-collar, working class kids.

Injured and muddy, cold and wet, the Madison players began walking off the field slowly. Only one player remained. Bruce refused to leave and he seemed oblivious to everything and everyone around him. He was battered and muddy. He was down on one knee on the nine-yard line. Charlie saw him pounding his fist on the ground. "We had these guys beat! We had these guys beat!" yelled an angry Bruce.

Charlie could see Bruce's face from the sideline and knew his anger was raging. Bruce finally got up and began to pace back and forth. He looked at the goal line with his hands on his hips and shook his head in total disbelief. "I can't believe it. We should not have lost."

Charlie ran back onto the field to get Bruce. He realized that Bruce was caught up in his own blow-by-blow replay of the game and that he was angry. He yelled at Bruce, "Come on, man, we got to go. We have got to go."

Bruce yelled back, "One more minute. Just one more stinking minute and we would have beaten the State champions!"

Charlie knew Bruce better than most people. Not only was he a teammate, but he was one of Bruce's best friends. So, he draped his arm over Bruce's shoulder and slowly walked them off the field together—injured, muddy, wet, cold, feeling angry and disappointed. All of a sudden Bruce looked at his friend Charlie and said, "We didn't quit, man, we didn't quit."

This awareness served Bruce well as his purpose became clearer a few months later. It helped define who Bruce was becoming: a leader with vision, courage and perseverance, someone who wouldn't quit even when victory seemed impossible or when he wasn't supported by the people he trusted.

A PERSONAL CHALLENGE IS DECLARED

With the Montclair High School game behind him Bruce experienced another important turning point in his life. It occurred during a high school Civics Class field trip to the United Nations in New York City. The mood was festive during the bus ride into the City. Spirits were high. Many of the kids had never been into New York City and thought this trip was a big deal. All around Bruce he could hear comments like, "New York's cool! Look at that! Where's the Statue of Liberty and Central Park?"

He wasn't as awed by the trip as his friends and fellow classmates were. He had been into the City a few times with his parents and enjoyed the museums. Right at that time he felt isolated and he was totally in his head. His mind was racing with so many thoughts going on all at once he wouldn't have been surprised to see a hamster racing around on its wheel. All of the comments and chatter were just white noise to him.

As they entered the City he saw big, overpowering canyons of concrete and steel. The buildings were so tall that you had to look straight up to see the sky. Everyone moved incredibly fast, hustling and bustling from one place to the next. It was a cacophony of humanity, all sizes, shapes, colors and ethnicities. Street vendors sold pretzels and chestnuts and loudly hawked their goods. Smoke exhaust from all of the buses on the street hung in the air. All of his senses were engaged and the whole scene made a huge emotional impact. "This is a city that never sleeps," he thought to himself.

As the bus pulled up to the curb everyone was excited about disembarking. They were anxious to get going on this exciting new adventure. There it was, right in front of them, their destination: the United Nations! Everyone immediately headed toward the entrance and as they passed through the beautiful plaza they noticed the well-kept grounds. Bruce heard comments like, "I can't believe we're going into the United Nations building. It's so impressive with all of the different flags flying high from each country."

The day was beautiful and clear, a great day to be out of class and in New York City. While his friends were having fun, teasing and joking with one another, Bruce's mood was serious and somber. His thoughts continued to race and he thought, "I know that in a matter of hours there's a possibility that I'm going to see face to face—well, not exactly face to face, more like from the UN visitors' gallery, the highest ranking Communist: Premier Nikita Khrushchev of the Soviet Union. It had been rumored that he would be addressing the United Nations General Assembly today."

In spite of the beautiful day and the high energy and excitement of his friends, Bruce felt as though he would be going to an execution. He had never met or seen a Russian Communist before. His friends and classmates were oblivious and acted as if they were on some kind of picnic! "What's wrong with this picture? Don't these guys get what's going on?" he wondered.

He remembered his grandfather's warnings about the evils of Communism. He was very aware that the Soviets had achieved several major milestones in technology. He had done some research before the field trip and knew that their significant achievements included the launch of Sputnik One three years earlier, the first man-made satellite to orbit the earth, the launch of the space dog, Laika, in November of 1957 followed by other accomplishments in science and technology.

Khrushchev boasted that the Soviets would put the first man into space. Bruce was alarmed and thought, "Every American should understand this threat!"

He felt that national patriotism was at an all-time low and Khrushchev took every opportunity to ridicule the United States while he praised the greatness of Communism. He believed Khrushchev would take advantage of his time before the General Assembly to further his own plans and that he would also ridicule the United States.

Bruce was so keyed up anticipating what was going to happen that he was a little frightened. He thought, "I can't believe I might actually get a chance to see Khrushchev in person. He's a monster as far as I'm concerned. Why will this man be allowed to ridicule and insult my country on our own soil?"

Anxious and tense he felt as though he had become a tightly wound clock ready to burst! He braced himself as he anticipated a confrontation. He thought to himself, "I feel as if I'm about to enter the boxing ring facing one of the toughest opponents of my life. I wonder who's going to throw the first punch."

Bruce took this personally and thought, "This is the man that represents all things evil as far as I'm concerned. I've heard this all of my life."

He anxiously but quietly took his seat in the visitors' gallery. As he turned to the front of the room Bruce was surprised and thought to himself, "I can't believe it! There he is, the Soviet Premier. He's no more than one hundred feet in front of me."

Bruce froze and could only stare at the man. As he watched him Khrushchev did the unthinkable. He took his shoe off and banged it on the podium as he continued to insult the United States.

He couldn't believe the man's arrogance. He listened to the Premier's translation carefully through the headphones that were provided to the visitors. "America's youth are weak and stupid and the Soviet's youth are strong and intelligent."

As far as Bruce was concerned the first punch was thrown. It felt like getting hit below the belt or in the head with a two-by-four. All that went through his mind was, "I am not weak or stupid. You don't know who you are messing with!"

With his head and thoughts reeling Bruce thought to himself, "Game on! You took your punch and now it's my turn!"

An uncontrollable fury burned in Bruce. He couldn't listen anymore. He was so upset and angry that he ripped the headset off of his head and threw it down on the floor. "I can't take listening to his garbage anymore," he thought. "Khrushchev's challenge is personal as far as I'm concerned. He's gone too far!"

In that moment Bruce made a silent and personal vow to himself and his grandfather: "I will make Khrushchev EAT HIS WORDS! I don't know how, but I will make it happen."

As he continued to sit in the visitors' gallery he was in his own private world. He tuned out everything and everyone. Before he knew it his friends, trying to get his attention, poked him and said, "Hey, man, come on. Let's hit the streets and have some fun."

That was the last thing Bruce wanted to hear. He was still fuming. He wasn't interested in having fun. All he thought about was Khrushchev and his threats. "This is very personal and I know that I've just encountered a very strong and formidable adversary."

"Come on, man, it's time to go. We have to leave the gallery now. The speakers are taking a break," explained his friend Charlie.

Bruce finally tuned back in to what was going on around him and noticed his friends getting up to leave. He realized it was time to go. He was slow, still thinking about what he had just witnessed. He lagged behind his friends.

As he walked out of the gallery he wondered, "What am I going to do? I have to do something. I'm still so angry my head feels as though it's going to explode!"

He continued to tune his friends out as they made their way to the bus. Bruce kept to himself, wrapped up in his own thoughts. The bus ride was noisy and everyone around him laughed and joked. Loud music played in the background. The guy behind him wanted to get Bruce's attention so he held the radio up to Bruce's ear. Bruce was still angry about the encounter with the Soviet Premier and he thought, "Enough! I've had enough!"

He turned around and punched the radio out of the kid's hands so hard it went flying down the aisle and as he did he yelled, "Turn that radio down!"

His friends were stunned and didn't understand what was going on with him so they began to tease him more. They became very sarcastic and taunted Bruce with their comments: "What's the matter, Bruce? What's up with you? What's wrong with some music? Are you some kind of prima donna? Oooh, aren't we touchy? Look at the big baby."

These tough Jersey kids cut him no slack. Bruce was furious and wanted nothing to do with them. He couldn't explain what he felt or what was going on so he did the only thing he knew how to do. He attacked and yelled back: "How can you guys laugh and joke around? Didn't you hear what I heard today? Khrushchev said, 'Soviet kids are better and smarter than we are.'"

That didn't make an impression on anyone. Everyone continued to laugh as though nothing had happened. He heard one of the kids say, "So what? Who cares? Lighten up, Bruce."

"Who cares? That's the problem. I care," replied an angry Bruce.

He felt sick and was disgusted by his friends' reactions. "Don't they get it? Didn't they even listen to what was said today? They should be getting ready for battle instead of laughing and joking. What's wrong with them?"

He was still angry with Khrushchev and didn't understand why no one else was. After his outburst and confrontation everyone on the bus decided to leave him alone and it grew quiet. No one wanted to make him any angrier than he already was. The ride home was very subdued.

Feeling desperate, alone and isolated, surrounded by silence and in a state of mind he couldn't explain he thought, "Maybe Khrushchev was right. I can see the problem clearly and I don't understand why others can't. It's a chilling thought and I don't want to believe it. I don't know what I'm going to do or how I'm going to do it, but I will do something."

The seeds of his mission sprouted and began to grow. He was ready to take action even though his ideas still weren't clear. "I'm on my own and there isn't any help coming from anyone. I don't care if I have to do it by myself. There's no going back even if my friends won't listen. I won't give up!" he promised himself.

In spite of the resistance and opposition that Bruce perceived he decided to go forward even though it seemed like an impossible task. He put the panic attacks and fear behind him and with his head down he took the next step. Bruce felt alone in his quest yet he felt strong and determined to do something. His mission began to take shape. An act of one is all it would take and he was willing and driven to move forward even though the details of his mission weren't totally clear yet.

A DEFINING MOMENT

The third and last significant event that helped Bruce clarify his mission occurred during the same year, just before homecoming weekend and during football practice. Practice seemed to take on a life of its own. It was almost dark and the practice should have been over an hour earlier. Everyone was exhausted from running sprints. The field lights were on and you could see rain and snow swirling in the glow of the lights. A heavy mist enfolded the field and everything appeared gloomy. The air felt heavy as though fog had been swirling on the ground.

It seemed to the players that practice wasn't going to end at any time soon. The team kick-off return specialist pulled a hamstring muscle and limped off the field. Instead of ending practice the Coach called Bruce over and said, "Get back there and return kick-offs. He won't be playing tomorrow."

You could hear moans coming from all of the players. They were ready to hit the locker room and call it a day. It was Friday night. Practice had already run over one and a half hours. Everyone had stuff to do to get ready for tomorrow's homecoming game and dance. The Coach didn't care. He had a personal grudge against Chatham High School, the team they were scheduled to play the next day. They were another archrival and had won the prior year's game. Coach didn't want a repeat performance and he wanted to make sure the players understood how important this game was. "Get back on the field and kick that ball!"

Bruce couldn't believe what the Coach asked him to do. He was angry and felt betrayed. He thought, "What? He's kidding, right? Does this guy hate me? Why can't someone else run back kicks? What's wrong with the running backs sitting on the bench? Tight ends don't run back kicks. I hate running back kicks!"

Practice was especially tough and Coach seemed unusually hard. Unsatisfied he kept yelling for more and better play: "Get out there. Play full out. No slacking off."

Bruce was a leader on the team and considered himself a team player. Although he didn't agree with Coach he ran to get into position and all he could think about was, "We've just finished running wind sprints and some of us are probably dehydrated. We're all exhausted and heaving our guts out. What is he thinking? He's obviously in a bad mood."

The field was harder to see but Bruce got in position and took the next kick-off. He fought off tacklers and returned the ball to the twenty-five yard line. The next thing he heard was the Coach screaming, "That's not good enough. We will never beat Chatham if you continue to play like that. Do it again, as though you mean it this time!"

Bruce couldn't believe what he heard but he got ready for the next kick-off. He made the catch and took it one yard deep into the end zone so he dropped to his knee. The Coach went berserk and yelled, "We're not out here till six o'clock in the dark to take knees in the end zone. Now run it back!"

"Man, what's going on? I can't do anything right. This isn't even what I do. I don't return kick-offs or play special teams."

Bruce focused and was ready for the next kick-off. "I had better run with it," he thought.

He caught it on the five-yard line and began to run up the right sideline. He made it to the forty-yard line, and then cut to the middle, running down the left sideline. He thought, "I'm going all the way into the end zone. The way looks clear."

Suddenly he realized the kicker came out of nowhere and grabbed his shoulder pads. He was slowing down. Bruce tried to shake him off but before he could, he saw a wall of tacklers ready to hit him. All of a sudden there was a loud snap. It was heard echoing across the field. Bruce was furious. He felt his leg go numb and then he had a huge rush of pain! He was down and writhing on the field.

He was angry and in pain. "I'm a really good player, a wide receiver and linebacker. I don't play on special teams. Tomorrow is a big and important game and now I'm hurt. Thanks a lot, Coach!" he thought.

The Coach and trainers finally arrived on the field. "Don't move, Bruce. Get off of him slowly," his Coach yelled.

Bruce heard the trainer say, "It's a bad break, Coach. He needs to get to the hospital now! Get the life squad out here, NOW!"

A BLESSING IN DISGUISE

Just like that, in a flash, Bruce's world and life changed in one single moment. His leg was broken in two places. No homecoming game or dance for Bruce. No football scouts from Cornell University to see him play in this important game either. It was a major setback. All he could see for the foreseeable future was surgery, pain and traction in the hospital for a few days, then lots of recovery time that included crutches and no football!

It was Friday night by the time he got to the hospital when he was told he needed surgery. His Mom was with him as he went into surgery. Everything was a blur as he came out of surgery.

When he woke up Saturday morning his Mom was with him and stayed for most of the day. He was in a lot of pain and had nothing but time on his hands, time to think. He was angry with the Coach and thought, "I still don't understand what happened at practice yesterday. Now, because of the Coach I'm missing the biggest rival game and won't be going to the homecoming dance with my girlfriend. What was he thinking? Here I am lying in a hospital bed and my football career is over. What's up with that? This is like some bad dream because of my dumb Coach. I'm done. What am I going to do now? My whole sense of identity and purpose is gone. I've got to start over."

He continued to think, "My father's still out of town, but maybe it's okay for now. I'm not ready for a fight with my old man. He's going to really be angry!"

On Sunday Bruce's teammates showed up at the hospital. He heard them laughing and joking as they came into his hospital room. All of them wore their letterman jackets and couldn't wait to tell Bruce the news. Charlie said, "Hey, good to see you, man. We beat Chatham!"

The senior captain came to present the game ball to Bruce. Quickly all you could hear was play-by-play game moves from the night before. It was important to Bruce. He knew the Chatham players well. Lots of laughing and celebrating went on all around his bed. Before long the guys left.

After the guys left Charlie stayed behind and asked, "How are you really doing, man?"

Bruce rolled his eyes and said, "What do you think?"

"Just checking. There's something I need to tell you. Man, you're not going to like this but your girlfriend showed up at the dance last night with some guy from Morristown."

Bruce felt as if he'd taken another blow to his gut. He felt betrayed and dishonored at a whole new level. "What? You've got to be kidding me?"

"No, man. We took care of it though," replied Charlie.

"What do you mean, you took care of it?" asked Bruce.

"No one spoke to her at the dance. We take care of our own, Bruce. She left early because everyone turned their backs on her and we got the guy alone outside and roughed him up a bit. That's how we look out for our own, man," explained Charlie.

Charlie finally left and Bruce felt disappointed and depressed. "Things can't get any worse than this," he thought.

Just then he heard a noise outside in the hallway. He looked up and saw his girlfriend standing in the doorway of his hospital room. This was the last straw! Bruce yelled for the nurses, "Throw her out! I don't want to see you or talk to you!"

She tried to reason with him and explain her side of the story but he wanted nothing to do with her and he wasn't open to listening to her. She said, "You don't understand."

"I don't want to listen to your excuses. Nothing you can say or do will change my mind," he responded.

As far as he was concerned she had betrayed him and nothing justified her actions. "It's over," he said with finality.

Crying, she turned and ran leaving Bruce alone in his room. He began to rationalize his situation and thought to himself, "What are girls anyway? Girls are a distraction! Now I can focus on what's important."

He wondered, "Now what am I going to do? I'm not an active jock anymore and I don't even have a girlfriend."

Then he began to worry about his father. "What am I going to tell him? He's been out of town and he didn't want me to play football in the first place. He's going to kill me!"

Bruce's Dad was stern and tough, a "take no prisoners" kind of man. He was on the road and away from home a lot as a Regional Sales Manager for a large pharmaceutical company. Bruce convinced his Mom to agree to sign the papers to let him play football this season. He realized that his Mom and Dad didn't have secrets, but his father had never come to one of his games. Now what?

Bruce was still in the hospital and it was Sunday evening. He had been sleeping and when he woke up there he was, in the flesh, his father, bigger than life, large and intimidating. He felt his disapproval immediately and cringed under the look he gave him. No sympathy or compassion was coming from this man. He was angry.

His father's anger was palpable and directed at him. He knew that if "looks could kill" he was already dead. He simply stared looking down at Bruce lying in his hospital bed, beat up and in a cast. Without saying one word to him, his father turned around and walked out of the hospital room leaving Bruce feeling devastated.

Talk about feeling all alone—in that moment all Bruce felt was pain, physical and emotional. Alone with his thoughts he wondered, "How am I supposed to fulfill my mission? I thought I knew. It's time to re-evaluate and re-define who I am and how I'm going to move forward with my life. I won't be getting a football scholarship to Cornell either. How can I make lemonade out of these lemons? What am I going to do?"

As he closed his eyes and began to drift off to sleep he remembered a ride home with his Dad a year earlier after the Chatham game. They talked about overcoming adversity. It seemed just like yesterday. Bruce played for Chatham as a freshman and ironically after moving a year later played for Madison against Chatham as a sophomore.

He remembered everything about the conversation on the drive home. The weather was dreary, wet and cold and by the end of the game it was raining so hard you couldn't see out of the car window. Madison lost at the last minute and Bruce took a lot of verbal abuse from his former Chatham teammates and friends. He remembered some of their mean and cutting comments: "Why are you playing for Madison? You're a traitor, Bruce."

Bruce wasn't the only one who heard the taunts. His father heard them too. Looking back Bruce saw how upset his father was as he watched the game. He saw Bruce hit and pushed after the play whistle sounded. He heard their mean and nasty remarks and saw the dirty looks aimed at Bruce, spitting on him as he walked by. All of the abuse was specifically aimed at his son, Bruce, whom they considered the enemy. The officials didn't do anything about it. "No wonder he didn't like me playing football," he thought.

On the drive home after the game he remembered that his father had tried to make small talk with him but he was so caught up in his own world he only responded with one-word answers. After a while his Dad gave up and grew silent, no longer looking over at Bruce at all. The silence was almost painful. All you could hear was the back-and-forth swishing of the windshield wipers—back and forth, back and forth. The sound was hypnotic and mesmerizing.

Then Bruce remembered his Dad suddenly pulled off the road and stopped. "What's going on?" he asked.

Ready for a confrontation his Dad said, "Hey, Bruce, do you want to know what the measure of a real man is?"

Bruce said, "Yeah."

His Dad went on: "Anyone can look good when times are good but the measure of a real man is how well he behaves when faced with real adversity. That's when your true nature comes out and you know what you're made of."

At sixteen Bruce didn't fully understand or appreciate his father's wisdom; however, it stuck with him for the rest of his life. He was so self-absorbed he suddenly realized what a jerk he was and said, "Thanks, Dad, thank you. I'll remember that."

The tone and mood in the car immediately shifted and lightened up.

Bruce wondered if this was why his Dad didn't want him to play football this year. He thought, "Maybe it's because he saw how badly I suffered from my former teammates and friends."

He thought more about it and continued to think about what kind of lemonade he could make. He remembered the silent vow he made to his grandfather, the vow he made during

Khrushchev's UN visit. After all, the seeds were planted years before by his Grandpa Joseph and now they were ready to grow. He wondered, "Is this accident really a blessing in disguise? Without football and my girlfriend I won't be distracted."

During the remainder of his hospital stay he obsessed about his new mission. All he thought about was finding a way to stop Nikita Khrushchev. "Man, how am I, a sixteen-year-old kid, going to beat the Soviets at their own game?"

His mission became clearer every day. After three days he left the hospital. "Man, I still don't have a clue about how to get it done."

"First things first," he thought. "I have to face my father when I get home. I'm not looking forward to that confrontation."

Bruce only saw roadblocks and obstacles ahead. He couldn't see an end in sight or any way around all those obstacles. "I've got to be tough. This isn't a pie-in-the-sky dream. I know this mission is achievable. It has to happen. It is necessary. No one can stop me, not even my angry father."

Bruce felt he had to make choices that were right for him, so, with a new determination and focus, when he returned to school he set out to learn everything he could about his adversary, the Soviets and their space and science programs. The school library became his sanctuary and his new best friend. It didn't take him too long to realize that his high school library had limited resources.

He remembered that Drew University was about four miles from his school. It was a beautiful, small Ivy League-like school that appeared to be a small version of Harvard. It had a fairyland quality about it and gas lamps lit the walkways on the campus. A plan began to form and Bruce thought, "I'm big and I can pass for a college junior. I bet I can get into Drew's library. I know it's bigger and has more information."

He decided after school to try and get into Drew University's library. It was cold this time of year and drifting snow was covering the streets and sidewalks as he headed there. He thought about his plan all of the way: "I'm not afraid to talk to people. I know the safest way to blend in is to be friendly. Girls seem to be easier to make friends with than guys."

He walked across the small campus and found the library. He saw an attractive young woman in front of the library. She looked as if she worked there. Bruce thought, "I'll talk to her. I need to make her my friend. She can help me get into the library with no problem."

He walked up to her and started to talk to her. He asked lots of questions. He improvised, adapted and stayed focused during his conversation. He overcame all of her objections as they talked. Finally, he convinced her that he needed a study carrel. She was reluctant at first because these were reserved for upper classmen. Bruce persisted and they became friends. She assigned him a study carrel too. "Now I can use the library whenever I want and do more extensive research. I also have the privacy here so no one questions why I'm here."

Bruce became so busy with his new interest and project that many of his old friends from the football team felt as though he had abandoned them. He wasn't considered by some to be one of the "cool jocks" anymore. This was uncharted territory as far as he was concerned. He didn't know where he fit in either. His teammates thought he acted weird. "Why aren't you at practice anymore? Do you think you're better than us?" he overheard them ask as they walked down the high school corridors.

"I don't fit in and I feel like a fish out of water. I'm not on the team anymore. Where do I fit?" Bruce wondered.

He had some choices to make. He felt shunned by his friends and thought, "If I've lost some of my teammates' respect, how do I get it back? Do I want it back?"

He didn't have the answers. He was cast adrift and felt alone in a sea of hundreds of kids. Half of the team didn't feel he belonged and he felt as though the nerds and intellects were afraid of him. Bruce was a smart guy but up until this point he never really applied himself. He did what was needed to get by. "Now what?" he asked himself.

After giving it some thought he decided to show up at a science club meeting. The "nerds" thought he was there to spy on them or play tricks on them. This was the history they had had with "jocks" in their school. Bruce wasn't a nerd and didn't fit in anywhere; no one trusted him. He realized he was no longer part of a group and his friends and classmates were confused. So was he.

Bruce persevered and decided he had to prove he was smart too. He studied hard and found that chemistry was easy. As he brought his chemistry grades up to straight A's he entered a national chemistry competition and won!

He realized that he could do anything he set his mind to do. He began taking some of the "nerds" under his wing and offered them his protection. He became a champion of the underdogs at school. In Bruce's experience jocks didn't have any use for brainy kids; they thought they were weak.

Even though he no longer totally fit in with any group he still tried to find his place. Since the accident his life had changed. No one felt comfortable around this new Bruce. He didn't always feel comfortable with himself either.

In spite of the resistance and obstacles that he encountered his faith in himself and his mission remained strong. He still didn't know what the outcome would look like exactly, but he believed he could make things happen! He was ready to take a big leap of faith against all odds!

AGAINST ALL ODDS

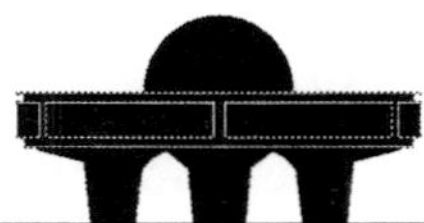

"Man, I can't win. Everything's so hard and I have to fight for every inch of progress. My whole life's changed and nothing's the same. I feel like a fish out of water and on top of everything else I don't fit in anywhere," thought Bruce. "I'm not ready to give up!"

Bruce had a vision of what he wanted to do but he didn't know how to do it! Even his parents didn't support him. His friends thought he was weird and had totally lost it. He was definitely a different person since he broke his leg and couldn't play football. Sometimes they looked at him as if he came from another planet!

Bruce's injuries were healing and he was off of his crutches and in a walking cast. He was sitting in homeroom class when his teacher came over and said, "Bruce, your Coach wants to see you in his office after school."

"Thanks," Bruce responded.

After school Bruce headed over to the Coach's office walking through the team locker room to get there. All of the players were suiting up for practice. Bruce felt a lot of mixed emotions coming from his friends and teammates. Some were really glad to see him but others made cutting comments: "Hey, man, look who's here! Yeah, it's the biggest, no, the largest nerd in school. Sure nice to see you, Einstein."

Bruce continued walking to the Coach's office and tried to ignore the comments. He didn't want to get into any hassles.

When he reached the office and walked in the Coach got right to the point and said, "Where have you been? Why aren't you out on the practice field anymore? You know you are letting your teammates down! You know that, don't you?"

"No, I'm not, Coach," responded a surprised Bruce.

"Yes, you are, and I'm the one saying you are, Tully!" yelled a heated Coach.

"No, I'm not," replied Bruce emphatically. "What I'm trying to do for my team is a lot more important than standing around on the sidelines every day, Coach!"

Coach didn't want to hear what he considered were excuses so he said, "That's it! You're done! Get out of here. You can kiss your letter for this year 'good-bye.'"

Bruce stopped and turned around. He looked his Coach squarely in the eyes and said, "Do what you have to do, Coach. I know I will."

He left his Coach standing there and made his way back through the locker room. He wasn't in any mood to talk to anyone. He was upset and angry and thought to himself, "Who is that guy? I've been loyal and I have given this team everything I've got. Doesn't he understand I have something better to do than stand out there on the sidelines? How can he take away a letter that I have more than earned? I don't get it!"

Before he could get out of the locker room he was stopped by DeAngelo, the running back. "Hey, what did Coach say?" DeAngelo asked.

"He said I'm out, done, and I won't get any varsity letter this year," replied Bruce feeling angry and disillusioned.

"Wow! Really?" asked DeAngelo.

"Yeah, really," growled Bruce.

DeAngelo decided to justify the Coach's position and asked, "Well, where have you been anyway? Everyone on the team says you've lost it since you broke your leg."

Bruce ignored his question and said, "Tommy, do you like milk?"

"What? What kind of answer is that?" asked DeAngelo.

"Just answer my question," responded Bruce.

"No, I don't like milk," DeAngelo answered.

"Have you ever tasted it?" asked Bruce.

"No, I just don't like it," DeAngelo replied.

Bruce continued to push DeAngelo and said, "That's my point, Tommy. That's just stupid. How do you know that you don't like milk if you've never tasted it before? Do you want to be an engineer or a scientist?"

DeAngelo was getting angrier and fed up with Bruce's seemingly meaningless questions and responded, "No! Just leave me alone. Stop asking such stupid questions."

By this time Bruce and DeAngelo were almost nose to nose, each one pressing the other. Bruce yelled, "Well, maybe you should be! You sure spend enough time at your uncles' stupid garage working on your stupid car engine."

DeAngelo had reached his breaking point and shoved Bruce hard. "Shut up!" he yelled.

Bruce, looking for a fight by this time, pushed him back harder and yelled, "No, you shut up!"

They were shoving and pushing each other, getting more and more physical the way things get resolved in New Jersey. The other players just watched and stayed out of it.

Charlie, Bruce's best friend and a hard-nosed tough guy, listened to the whole thing while he suited up for practice. Finally he had had enough. He stepped in, not wanting anyone to get hurt, and demanded, "No, you both shut up!"

Charlie's intervention surprised both Bruce and DeAngelo. No one messed with Charlie. So, DeAngelo pushed away, put on his helmet and stormed out of the locker room.

Charlie corralled Bruce and walked with him out of the locker room. He turned to Bruce and said, "Man, you've sure changed since your injury. All this stuff with the nerds is different. You're always in study hall or the library now. We never see you anymore. My cousin said she saw you over at Drew University in the library last week. What's up with that?"

Bruce responded, "Yeah, I fooled them into thinking I was a student there. They gave me a study carrel and a library card. I've got my own little room to work in now. They usually only give them to seniors. I sweet-talked a cute student assistant into giving me one. She thinks I'm in college."

"Well, you're big enough and smart enough to be in college," responded a laughing Charlie.

Bruce began to laugh too, enjoying Charlie's comment. "What's this stuff all about anyway?" Charlie asked.

Bruce thought for a moment and searched for the right words trying to explain: "I'll let you know, man, when I figure it all out myself. You had better get to practice or you will be running laps. I don't want that happening on my account. Thanks, Charlie."

Charlie gave Bruce a nod of assurance and hustled out of the locker room and headed for the practice field.

As Charlie left Bruce continued to think about what had happened with the Coach. "He still expects me to stand on the sidelines at every practice in spite of my injury. I've always supported Coach and the team. I've been loyal, but I guess it's not enough. Coach thinks I'm betraying him and the team. What a crock! This is so unfair!"

He was disappointed, disillusioned and felt betrayed by his Coach and some of his teammates. Bruce began to harden his feelings: "I guess I'm still all alone in this. DeAngelo is Coach's favorite and he's the guy I covered for when I broke my leg. Man, I refuse to let this get me down. I know I'm not worthless. I'll show them what's more important than standing on the sidelines of a football field."

He had a vision and a mission. Something burned within him. He had a feeling that kept urging him to take the next step, whatever it was. He knew he had to keep moving forward. Some people describe this as a gut feeling or intuition. Bruce didn't know why. He just knew he had to keep going, one step at a time. He still wasn't clear about what he was going to do or how he was going to do it.

He continued to research his adversary, the Soviet Union. He also wanted to know what the "nerds" at school felt about their futures. He asked some of them: "What do you want to do after high school? How do you plan to get it done?"

At first they were leery of Bruce and didn't trust him. He had never shown any interest in them before. Bruce discovered that these kids were clear and motivated. They made a big impression on him.

One of the kids admitted, "I want to be a nuclear physicist and, if I could have one wish, it would be to talk to Dr. Edward Teller, the father of the H-bomb. That's my dream."

Someone else told Bruce, "I want to speak with Dr. Wernher von Braun, the German rocket scientist who is leading the emerging U.S. space program. I know this will never happen."

These kids' dreams made a great impact on Bruce and an idea began to form. It still wasn't fully clear but he felt he was getting closer. The feeling deep within him kept urging him onward.

During his research he realized that other countries were far more committed to space and science programs for students than the U.S. He found that Germany offered a two-week-long science fair where students and top scientists interacted with one another. "This is great and a step in the right direction," he thought to himself. "The United States of America is the greatest free country in the world and we don't have any programs like this! We aren't even close. The Soviets ARE winning and Khrushchev was RIGHT!"

He kept asking himself, "How can I make a difference? I'm just one sixteen-year-old high school student, a kid. What can I do?"

He felt at a standstill. "Where do I begin?"

All of a sudden he knew how to approach the problem. Like most kids his age he watched TV and enjoyed detective shows. So he imagined he was a detective and looked at the basic yet looming question again. He asked himself, "Why does Khrushchev think that his kids are better than us? What are they doing that we aren't?"

He kept running this question through his mind over and over again until his head was spinning. It was a beginning and it helped him focus his research. He had moments of doubt along the way, however, and he continued to wonder and ask himself, "How am I going to pull this off?"

One thing remained clear to him through all of his self-doubt. The vision and mission of his research never changed. He was determined to discover if Russian kids were better than American kids.

Bruce was physically healed and he sat in his new favorite place, Drew University library, his own private room. His mind wandered as he thought about spring. He couldn't believe how much research information he had collected and wondered how he was going to make sense of it. "How does all of this fit into my mission?" he asked himself.

It was while he sat there brainstorming that ideas began to crystallize for him. He realized that Russia and the United States were governed in totally different ways. He began to see that because of this difference most Russian kids didn't have choices or a voice in their futures. The State decided who went to school and what schools they attended. In the U.S. everyone could decide their own futures and make their own choices.

He started to compare the two countries even more and realized that Russia was highly structured and organized. They had a selection process. Kids were focused in areas where they were perceived to have talent and strength. Once this was identified the kids received the appropriate training and education. Kids were put into immersion programs and usually they didn't have a choice or a voice. They did what they were told.

United States kids, on the other hand, have lots of choices and can make them freely. Bruce recognized that in order for a kid in the U.S. to specialize or to be interested in science or technology some way to capture that kid's interest had to develop. In some ways it appeared that U.S. kids looked for immediate gratification and lost interest easily.

Bruce continued to sort out and organize his thoughts and the information he remembered from his conversations with the school "nerds." These kids, although interested and motivated, felt hopeless. They didn't see any way to accomplish their dreams and to meet key scientists and innovators. They were left to their own devices to discover ways to get the training, support and education that would help them live their life dreams. Bruce thought to himself, "It seems as if freedom is working against us."

His imagination began to take over and he became obsessed with finishing his project. He recalled the times that he went to New York with his parents and had visited the Hayden Planetarium and the American Museum of Natural History. These visits began to fuel the mental pictures that were forming in his mind.

He went to the front desk at the library and asked his friend, "May I borrow a typewriter?"

Bruce felt he was ready to get all of the thoughts and ideas out of his head. It was time to write down a solution for what he saw as the problem. The United States was behind in the space race and American students were not competitive in the areas of science and technology. The Soviet Union was currently leading in both the space race and in student development for the studies of science and technology. Where to begin?

THE *MANIFESTO* IS CREATED

Bruce understood that his thoughts had to be clear as he developed his plan with no distractions. So he focused and began to write what he called his *Manifesto*! This was a document that described what he thought the problem was and what a proposed solution would be—a huge undertaking as far as he was concerned. He was determined, dedicated and diligent as he wrote and rewrote his *Manifesto*. Finally, he finished!

Manifesto

From the beginning of time mankind has reached out to grasp the future and understand the happenings which were to take place in our universe. But how few of us actually do that? Unfortunately, only a select few are able to understand, witness and be a part of the processes of progress, much less contribute something toward these achievements which must continue.

Progress cannot be stopped, and we must be ready and active to take part in this changing world.

Today this world of ours is on the verge of a new era, the "Space Age," which opens vistas in many wonderful and fascinating fields. We are on the threshold of the conquest of many problems which have plagued mankind down through the centuries. Scientific achievements are going to be greater than ever.

However, the problem facing our country today is the lack of trained young people (or old, for that matter), who can carry the banner of progress forward. We may ask, "Is this due to disinterest in our young people?" No, that is not the answer at all.

Today and every day many young people do not use the untapped talents within themselves. They live from one day to the next without accomplishing much or contributing their rightful share toward the fast-paced, ever-changing scene. In the United States, and undoubtedly throughout the world, we have numerous young men and women who could be leaders in their fields if we could find them and develop them. The brilliant minds must be captured in their youth and their sparks of interest fanned into flames to bring greater discoveries for the good of all.

Many of our youths in high schools and colleges do not know exactly to what they want to devote their lives. When asked, "What career would you like to follow when you graduate?" they cannot answer immediately. Some have no answer at all, and perhaps never will.

What is the cause of this apathetic attitude on the part of our young people? The answer is relatively simple. They have, really, very little opportunity to be exposed to the vast well of information available today. No place is available for the young men and women to see firsthand just what research, industry and science are achieving. If they could see some of the fantastic accomplishments of our great industries and sciences today, a new army of future men and women of science would expand, an army which is badly needed by our country and the world.

The purpose of the proposed Astronarium and Science Center is to bring industry and science to the youth of today, to stimulate their minds and create interests in fascinating futures.

By elaborate displays, lectures, classes and programs supplied by the government and industry, information heretofore unattainable anywhere else in the world will be brought to these young people firsthand in one building and under one roof. The seed of curiosity in science can be planted forever, for their own and their country's futures.

The proposed Astronarium and Science Center will not only be for the benefit of our youth, but also for the benefit of all ages. Here will be obtained firsthand information on what our nation is doing in the new fields of science and technology. When this vast quantity of knowledge is revealed, subjects that were only read about in the newspapers and magazines and really not fully understood will be explained and demonstrated. When leaving the Center, the public will have learned firsthand about these new accomplishments. As a result of all this, a higher respect for the nation and the nation's industries will be gained, for they will be assured that the United States is still the world's leader in the fields of science and technology.

Industries will benefit also as a result of the new Astronarium and Science Center. The industries that display their newest works in the Center will be showing the nation and the world what they can do and what they are doing. As a result, these industries will gain greater prestige and respect among the people, for the people will see and know that each of these industries is genuinely contributing to the progress of the nation and the world.

Companies that exhibit in the Center will receive the benefit of a vast amount of the untapped brainpower of those young people who have come to the new Center, who have seen and learned from the displays and who have headed into a career of science and technology. These same companies will not only arouse interest in their products but also in the expansion of those corporations, and further development of their products, by capital investment.

The area which is chosen for the erection of the proposed Astronarium and Science Center will also benefit. It will act as a tourist center for people from all over the world. Since there is nothing like this in the world today, people

*will come to see this vast new lecture and demonstration
hall, sit in the world's largest and best-equipped Astronarium and see shows never shown in the world before. It will
not only benefit the State, its industries and its students,
but it will serve as an inspiration in the fields of science
and technology for the nation and for the world.*

He felt good and he was excited. "I've done it. It's done.
I can't believe it! My vision and mission are crystal-clear and
I have something to show people."

He could see in his mind's eye exactly how it looked. He
wasn't restricted or limited in what he imagined and
thought. "I want a *Temple of Knowledge* to be created and I
will call it *The Astronarium and Science Center*. Astronarium
is a new word that I made up. It combines parts of the words
Astronautics, Astronauts and Planetarium. These three
words symbolize all of the pieces that are included. Okay, so
now what do I do with all of this?"

He thought about his approach and decided that the next
step was to design and build a scale model of what he saw
in his mind's eye, a Hayden Planetarium on steroids! "It will
be bigger and more dramatic—a science center but so much
more. I can see kids having interactive experiences within
the Astronarium. A knowledge center will be there where
you can listen to lectures from the world's top scientists and
even access them from your home TV. You will be able to see
missions to the moon!"

In that moment Bruce became a young visionary with a
clear mission. His enthusiasm for what he had imagined

created an excitement within him that he could hardly contain. "This could be the spark that ignites the awakening flames for millions of kids. It could help the United States become a leader in space and technology. Now how am I going to develop a set of mechanical drawings and build a scale model of my project?"

THE VISION AND THE MISSION TAKE FORM

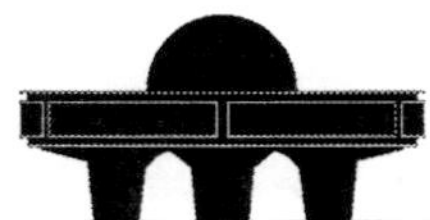

Bruce was ready to take his ideas, what he could see in his mind's eye, and create drawings and a model to show people. He knew that his parents weren't going to help him since his Mom was working and taking care of his brother and sister and his Dad was on the road traveling with his job. So, in order to build a model Astronarium he would have to make do with resources that he had on hand. The only things he found to draw with were pencils and rulers. He didn't have extra money to purchase drafting tools and he didn't have any mechanical drawing training.

He was determined and didn't let this stop him from moving forward with his project. Once again he drew on his own inner resources and imagination and decided to work on the drawings late at night after his parents had gone to bed.

In his mind's eye he saw an exhibit hall with a ring around it, circular and spherical like the early space stations. In some ways it reminded him of a doughnut with a center and spokes radiating outward, a space station on the ground.

"It's hard enough to draw something with straight lines and angles. Circles are impossible!" Bruce mused.

He made a trip to the local office supply and found a "beam compass" that could make huge circles. "This is just what I need," he thought.

He checked the price and saw a fifty-dollar price tag. "No way can I afford this. Mom and Dad aren't going to pay for it either. All I can afford is the professional drafting paper," he realized.

He was disappointed and then his imagination began to go wild. He wondered what he could use to draw big circles instead. He grew more frustrated every day. Nothing seemed to work. He needed a circle that was big, something he could use to draw his design. It took days before he had an idea.

It came to him while he watched his mother cooking one evening in the kitchen. He saw a large pan with a large lid and then he saw smaller pans and lids. "These can all fit inside the larger ones. Of course! Everyday pots and pan lids! I can use them to draw my floor plans which will serve as a basis for my model."

Bruce sat in the kitchen later that evening. He was ready to draw his design using the pan lids at a size and scale that could eventually be built. He thought, "I can improvise. I'm not a quitter. So, I will make do with what is on hand."

Pot lids and yard sticks became the tools of his trade. The kitchen table became his drafting table. His imagination went into overdrive as he tried to be quiet and not wake up his parents. He explored every cupboard and cabinet, every pot and pan lid in his mother's kitchen. He realized he had to adapt to what was available. He couldn't afford to buy professional tools. He began to see size and scale relationships and reasoned that he could approximate a scale using different-sized pots and pan lids.

He found a yardstick and got out his pencils. All of a sudden without realizing it he was using algebraic formulae and processes to solve the problems without any training. He had paper and in his dimly lit kitchen, sitting all alone, he began to draw a primitive two-dimensional set of architectural drawings. It wasn't easy, being quiet.

At one point his Mom came out and asked, "What are you doing?"

Bruce responded, not wanting to go into a lot of detail, "A project for school."

He kept his response short. Sitting alone in the kitchen he completed his first set of drawings, giving them his best efforts with what he had on hand.

Bruce's vision was clear and he was focused—a man on a mission. He was single-minded and determined to get the drawings and model finished but realized he needed help. Bruce recognized that if he was going to get this project done he needed support from two key teachers. He was clear about what he needed each one of the teachers to do. All he had to do was figure out how to convince them to help him.

He realized that his first set of drawings was rough and thought, "I need to create a better set of three-dimensional drawings that includes plans, elevations from street level and section views. It seems overwhelming. Once I finish them, then I will need a scale model of the Astronarium. It can be built from the detailed drawings."

With his plan clear in his mind he decided to approach Madison High's mechanical drawing teacher even though Bruce wasn't in his class.

Since he was so determined to make his vision real he searched for people who could help him. "I won't take 'no' for an answer," thought a determined Bruce, "even if they tell me I can't work on my project instead of going to study hall."

Eventually, through his persistence and clear vision, the mechanical drawing teacher agreed to let him work on refining his drawings in class instead of having a study hall period.

Next he had to find a way to build a scale model of his design. Bruce approached the wood shop teacher. Once again he met resistance. What he wanted to build in shop class wasn't part of the curriculum. High school juniors were supposed to build knick-knack shelves for their mothers. Bruce didn't let this discourage him.

He began to think about overcoming the shop teacher's objections: "How can I make this work for both of us?"

Suddenly the answer was clear. He realized that the only requirement for the class project was that it had to be built from plans and that it had to be made of wood. He could do this!

Finally Bruce convinced the teacher that his project would meet these requirements. Suddenly he had the green light to move forward and create a model of what he saw in his mind's eye.

It wasn't going to be quite that easy he found out.

When you think you have everything lined up and that you are ready to go sometimes unforeseen events happen. This was true for Bruce. He learned in a very significant way through his football experience that people he trusted let him down. As his project was moving forward he found new obstacles to overcome.

CHOICES, CONSEQUENCES AND REWARDS

He was like a man possessed, diligently working to take his vision and create a design and model. Finishing was all he thought about. "I feel as if I have the answer to Khrushchev's challenge. It's right there! I have to keep going," he reminded himself.

Every waking moment was spent on his project and it became all-consuming. Each day looked the same: wake up, eat and breathe nothing but his project. Occasionally he gave in to sleep.

As he diligently worked on his design and model the Soviet Union continued to make international headlines on a daily basis. This really bugged him.

Time seemed to pass quickly and suddenly it was 1960 and springtime. Now the Soviets claimed they shot down one of our U-2 spy planes. "I can't believe what I just read," declared a furious Bruce. "There's a greater sense of urgency now and I have to finish this! I've got to do this. Political activities are getting out of hand!"

He felt a sense of desperation and asked himself, "What's next? We have no choice anymore. We're doomed."

"This is no longer something that's nice to do. We need it to happen at a national level," thought a worried and determined Bruce. "I need more time. Where will it come from?"

He did the unthinkable in spite of harsh and unbelievable consequences. "I'm going to cut some of my classes so I can finish. I know that cutting classes isn't a minor infraction of the school rules. It's way more serious than confiscating a transistor radio. This is a big deal and might get me suspended from school. What will my parents do if that happens? Still, I have to finish this, no matter what."

Having made his decision, he proceeded to cut classes. One day he was tracked down by the Dean of Men who liked to rove the school halls looking for kids who weren't doing what they were supposed to be doing. Bruce took a deep breath and knew it was time to pay the piper.

The Dean of Men said roughly, "Mr. Tully, let's you and I visit the Principal's office right now."

Bruce realized he had no choice but to go along. As he walked with the Dean he thought, "I'm done for. This idiot is narrow-minded and self-serving. My project is going to end up in the trash. What more can happen? All of my noble work is going to be destroyed by someone who doesn't understand at all how much it is needed. I've made so much progress. This can't be happening. I feel as though I have entered the twilight zone!"

They arrived in the Principal's office together. The Dean had already confiscated his project materials. Bruce's thoughts were racing: "This is a disaster. The Dean would love to destroy all of my work. He's always wanted to get me. He would love to make an example out of me in front of the whole school. Just because I've been the leader and part of "voices for action" and we've made fun of some of the dumb rules that he's put in place, I can't let this happen. What am I going to do?"

He watched the Dean hand over all of his hard work to the Principal and he held his breath. He listened as the Dean told the Principal that he had been caught cutting class. "We need to do something about Bruce's breaking of the school rules," postulated the Dean.

As far as the Dean was concerned all Bruce had was a pile of junk worth nothing. Bruce tuned out the conversation between the Dean and Principal. He couldn't believe he had been caught. "I'm so close to finishing. I wonder what the Principal is going to say and do. Man, what's my Dad going to do to me if I get suspended?"

He tuned back in to what was being said as the Dean continued his recommendation to the Principal, "The rules are simple. First, I recommend three days' suspension, then a conference with Bruce and his parents before he comes back to school. Confiscate all of this junk and then give him heavy after-school detention since this isn't Mr. Tully's first offense."

Bruce thought to himself, "He hates me. I don't regret organizing the football team's response to the school's stupid "no jeans in school" rule or "boys must wear ties to school" rule. In fact, I loved seeing fifty kids show up at school, all of us wearing five- to eight-foot long ties dragging on ground!"

He realized that these actions to poke fun at the rules which resulted in extra detention and paperwork for the Dean didn't make him the Dean's friend. The Dean knew that Bruce was the instigator behind all of the stunts and he resented him. He could almost feel the Dean's thoughts of victory: "I've got you!"

Bruce heard the Principal address him directly, "What do you have to say for yourself this time, Bruce? Is there any good reason for me not to suspend you and confiscate your materials?"

Taking a deep breath Bruce replied respectfully, "Sir, I have something for you to read. Will you please read my paper? I know it will help explain why I was cutting class to work on my project."

The Principal looked at Bruce and with his curiosity piqued he took the paper and said, "Let me see it."

Quickly Bruce handed over his *Manifesto* and anxiously watched the Principal read his document.

While reading the Principal looked over at the Dean and said, "I'm afraid I'm going to have to consult with the Assistant Superintendent of Schools on this one. I will call him right away and see if he has time to join us and discuss this with Bruce. Until then, I'm going to wait to decide what we should do."

Bruce couldn't believe it. "I have been given a reprieve! What does it mean?"

He glanced over at the Dean who looked puzzled, confused and disappointed. Bruce felt like the weight of the world had been lifted from his shoulders, as if a death sentence had been commuted by the Governor. The meeting was over for now.

He thought as he walked out, "My parents don't understand my vision or the scope of my project. They definitely won't understand it if I am kicked out of school. They haven't taken the time out of their own busy lives to understand what I'm doing."

He breathed a sigh of relief and headed for home but he was restless and didn't sleep well that night. He didn't want to tell his parents that he was in trouble either. The last thing he remembered as he finally began to drift off to sleep was, "I wonder what tomorrow will bring and I wonder who this Assistant Superintendent is?"

On the way to school the next morning he tried to put his conflicts and differences with the Dean of Men out of his mind: "The Principal seems like a nice guy. I still wonder who this guy is that he wants me to meet. I guess I'm going to be judged by someone I don't know. I don't think I'm out of the hot water yet."

Sitting in class the next morning he was summoned once again to the Principal's office. He took a deep breath and wondered, "Now what? I guess I'm going to have to try and convince a total stranger what I'm doing is important for our country. My fate is being decided by three people it seems. I don't have any control here. I hate feeling helpless with other people in charge."

He left the classroom and hustled to the Principal's office. He knocked on the door and was greeted by the Assistant Superintendent of Schools! This meeting happened faster than he expected. Bruce looked at him and saw an educated, dignified, elderly and kind gentleman in front of him. He began to relax immediately and thought, "This is someone I can trust. I don't know how I know it but that's what I feel. I'm glad I'm meeting with him and not just the Dean again."

Bruce didn't quite know what to expect from the Assistant Superintendent. He thought to himself, "This feels like judgment day and I know it can go a couple of ways. I will do my best to explain it. My mission is so clear to me and I feel it needs to be accomplished at all costs. I have to convince him how important it is to our nation. He looks interested."

"Why am I sitting across from a sixteen-year-old today?" asked the Assistant Superintendent. He invited Bruce to tell his story.

So Bruce began at the beginning and calmly outlined the events, explaining his thoughts in detail. The Assistant Superintendent listened to what he said and asked clarifying and probing questions. He was sincere and wanted to understand fully what was going on. Bruce respectfully answered all of his questions and as the discussion was ending the Assistant

Superintendent asked one last and very important question: "If the school allows you to finish this project, Bruce, what will you do with the completed work?"

This was his chance and Bruce quickly responded without any hesitation: "Sir, I will have a complete presentation to show anyone who will listen to me!"

"Yes, son, I realize that. How will you get people to listen to you and who will you present this to?" probed the Assistant Superintendent.

Bruce was quick to respond: "We live just thirty minutes, by train, to the greatest city in the world, New York City. School is almost out for the summer and I plan to take my proposal into the City and talk to anyone who will listen to me!"

"Are you really committed to this, Bruce? You know it won't be easy, don't you?" asked the Assistant Superintendent.

With a firm commitment and conviction in his voice Bruce said, "Yes, I am, sir, and I know it won't be easy!"

Satisfied with Bruce's response the Assistant Superintendent asked the Principal's secretary, "Please have the Dean and Principal join me and Bruce. I'm done here."

When both men arrived he addressed them: "Mr. Tully is to have our full support in finishing his work as quickly as possible. What he's trying to do is what I believe a public school education is all about. We should have more Bruce Tullys at Madison High School. We're finished here for today. Good afternoon, gentlemen!"

As he got ready to leave he turned to Bruce and said, "The school year is almost over and in about three weeks summer vacation will be here. Let me know how your trip to the City works out. I'm anxious to hear about your results."

"Yes, sir," replied Bruce.

The Principal thanked the Assistant Superintendent for his support and feedback and watched him walk out of the office, turn and close the door behind him. He turned to Bruce and the Dean and said, "I knew we would get a solution and I'm pleased with the results."

The Dean looked stunned and he was furious. His body language was tense. Bruce thought he might jump him at any minute. The Dean asked, "How am I ever going to do my job if I don't get supported?"

Then with a bit of a smirk on his face Bruce said, "May I go now?"

He left the Principal's office and felt vindicated. He thought to himself, "I feel like a million bucks. Yes, the Assistant Superintendent gets it! This is the first time I have been treated like an equal by any adult. He actually complimented me and recognized the importance of what I'm doing. I have never gotten this kind of support from my Dad. I have never lived up to his expectations."

Bruce felt hopeful and refreshed. He thought, "If I can convince the Assistant Superintendent of Schools, then I can convince others in New York City to listen to me. I can be heard. I have a story that's worth telling!"

THE MOMENT OF TRUTH

Bruce was relieved that school was out. It was time to get his parents' support for what he wanted to do for the summer. He wasn't looking forward to talking to his Dad about it though. It seemed as if their only interactions resulted in confrontations. His project was important and he was ready to move forward. He wondered, "How am I going to get them to support my plan? There's so much to do and think about. I need to get some travel guides and pictures of New York City to prepare for my mission. How do I get there? Going by train or bus seems like going across the country. This is a huge undertaking!"

He decided to talk to his Mom first. He thought, "We get along really well. I help her with the kids and around the house. She knows how to talk to my Dad and smooth things over."

He began to talk to his Mom giving her bits and pieces about his project and overall plan. When he was confident that she understood what it was about he knew he could count on her support.

So, after dinner one evening he faced the moment of truth. While they were still sitting at the kitchen table with the wonderful scents still lingering from his mother's cooking, Bruce knew this was it. It was time to talk about his plan for the summer. He needed both of his parents to agree to let him go into New York City alone without any escort. His Mom agreed to introduce the subject for him and she said, "Tell Dad about your plans for the summer, Bruce."

He began to tell his Dad about his project, how it came about. "I put the finishing touches on it before school was out. I want to contact people that are open to hearing my proposal in New York City," explained an excited but cautious Bruce.

He felt the tension in the room. His Dad's body language told him that there was no way it was going to happen. It was then that his Dad asked his Mom, "Has everyone gone nuts around here? There's no way he's going into the City alone; absolutely not!"

Bruce thought he was done for, defeated before meeting with one person. It couldn't happen. His Dad got up from the table almost knocking the chair over and he began to pace—back and forth, back and forth. He reminded Bruce of a caged animal who was ready to escape or strike out. Bruce knew not to say a word. Looking Bruce directly in the eye and with their noses almost touching he asked, "When did you come up with this stupid idea?"

Bruce tried to speak but his Dad just kept on talking. Nothing stopped him. "Who do you think is going to listen to you anyhow? You're just some stupid kid from New Jersey with some pipedream in his head. Why should anyone listen to you?"

Bruce felt pushed to his limit. He was angry and stood up knocking his chair over. He yelled back at his Dad: "What kind of father are you anyhow? You never came to any of my games. You never went to the school for anything, never! All you ever do is tell me I'm not as good as you are at anything. Now you want to stop me from doing this. Who are you anyhow?"

The anger was getting out of hand and going downhill. His Mom realized their angry expressions had gone too far. She quietly listened to the exchange and rarely raised her voice but when she did she always got results. She was able to calm tense situations as well as Bruce's Dad.

Finally she stood up, immediately getting their attention, and said, "Stop it! Stop it, both of you, right now." She looked Bruce's Dad in the eye and calmly said, "I will talk to you about this later."

Then she turned to Bruce and told him, "Go outside and wash your father's car. I don't ever want to hear you talk to him like that again! Do you understand me? He's your father and my husband. That's who he is! Now, get outside NOW!"

Exasperated and chastised, Bruce turned around and left the room still steaming about the confrontation with his Dad. After a little while he finally calmed down and thought, "I have to trust that my Mom can bring my Dad around."

Later that evening after everyone had calmed down Bruce was asked to come back into the kitchen and join his parents. They all sat at the kitchen table. Bruce's Mom looked at him and said, "Bruce, your father has something to say to you."

He looked at his Dad and wondered what he would say after the angry confrontation earlier in the day. Apparently his Dad had a change of heart. Bruce knew he had his Mom to thank for it.

He listened to his Dad lay down the rules: "You can go into the City, Bruce, but you only take the train into Grand Central and then get off in Midtown. You stick to Midtown, do you understand? You don't go Uptown or to the West Side. The gangs in New York City will eat you up! They will smell you out like fresh meat! So stick to the business district. Oh, and one more thing. You have to be home every night by 6:00 p.m. If you can't find your way home by that time, then it's over and you're done!"

His Dad wasn't finished. "Now I'm going to give you a map of Midtown Manhattan. The streets are marked and these are the boundaries that I told you about. Do you get it?"

Bruce could barely sit still. He was beaming like a Christmas tree all lit up! He happily responded, "Yeah, Dad, I get it!

His Dad still wasn't finished: "If you think you're going to see all of these big shots in Manhattan, then Mom says you need a new suit, shirt, ties and some other shoes besides your sneakers. Let's go. I'm taking you to K-Mart and we will get you some stuff."

So off they went. Three suits, three shirts, three ties and a pair of dress shoes later Bruce was ready to begin the next leg of his journey, a journey that would change his life forever. Not only would it change his life. It could impact his country! He thought he was only going to New York City. Little did he know!

THE MOMENT OF TRUTH 79

WELCOME TO
NEW YORK CITY

It was time for Bruce to take a big leap of faith. It was early the next morning and Bruce was excited. "This is the big day," he smiled.

He wasn't really hungry but he ate breakfast and could hardly contain his excitement. "Which suit shall I wear?" he wondered.

He dressed like a warrior ready to greet the business world in his new clothes and hopped in the car with his Mom. He was too excited and nervous to talk on the way to the train station. His proposal and his model were with him and he kept asking himself, "How am I going to juggle all of these things and still look professional? Where am I going? I don't have a clue. No doubt I will figure it out when I get there."

His Mom dropped him off at the Lackawanna train station in Madison, New Jersey. Before she left him she reminded, "Don't forget the time. You need to be back here on the 5:45 p.m. express train. It leaves Grand Central Station just before 5:00 p.m. Be on it!"

"Don't worry, Mom. I will be on it," he promised, reassuring her.

This was a first for Bruce. He was dressed in a suit and tie and looked like all of the other busy commuters. Everyone seemed to know what they were doing and where they were going. So much hustle and bustle was going on all around him that he wasn't sure exactly what to do. "I may look the part, but I have no clue how this all works," he thought to himself.

Bruce got his bearings watching the train come into the station. There was a big rush so he bought his ticket as everyone seemed to push and shove trying to board the train. Almost immediately it was ready to leave the station.

Once he made his way through the sea of commuters juggling all of his stuff without dropping any of it he saw people sitting in their seats eating doughnuts and reading newspapers. No one seemed interested in him or anyone else around them.

He took a deep breath and began to juggle his stuff while he moved down the aisle looking for a seat. He felt invisible. "It's like no one sees me. They are all in their own little worlds." He was jostled from side to side continuing down the aisle while trying not to drop anything.

Finally he found a seat at the back of the train and sat down. He looked out of the window and saw his Mom still standing anxiously on the platform. As the train pulled out of the station he waved "good-bye." For a moment he felt a sense of separation. He was leaving all that he knew and all that he was comfortable with behind. He realized that he was all alone and thought, "Be careful what you ask for! Welcome to the real world!"

Bruce decided to set aside his feelings of anxiety and tackle this trip like a new adventure. His mind began to race and excitement kicked in. He thought, "I'm really sitting here in this train and I'm on my way by myself to New York City! Now what am I going to do? Where am I going? Who am I going to see? Who's going to want to see me? How am I going to figure it out?"

He had no answers to his questions yet and his questions swirled around in his head as the train traveled closer and closer to Grand Central Station. It felt as though he had been traveling into the bowels of the earth and the tunnel smelled like soot. He began to panic. All of a sudden the reality of it all set in again and he began to have more doubts. Out of nowhere he remembered the wise words of his Grandpa Joseph who had faced real fear. "Fear will kill your head! When you are afraid, and you will be, you must face your fear head-on; then move forward into its face. Before you know it, Bruce, your fears will be behind you!"

Recalling these words brought feelings of calm and possibility. His panic began to go away. "I can do this. Thank you, Grandpa! Together we will go forward today and fight that murderer Khrushchev, just as I promised you I would."

Immediately Bruce A. Tully aka Boris Antonavich Tugliglowitz no longer doubted. He felt confident and sure of himself as he continued to think about his strategy once he reached New York City. His head was spinning with ideas and he wondered, "Where do I start?"

Ideas kept whirling around inside of his head but the answers never seemed quite clear. Soon they began to take on the rhythm of the train zooming toward New York City and the cadence and sound on the tracks: clickity-clack, clickity-clack, a steady rhythm lulling Bruce's senses.

Up ahead Bruce could see the tunnel that ran under the Hudson River. He knew that Grand Central Station was just on the other side. He returned to the task at hand. He gathered his briefcase and the model and he prepared to leave the train.

Bruce was nervous and excited at the same time. The train entered the dark tunnel and all of a sudden it felt very eerie. Sounds were heightened and the tunnel was so long Bruce wondered if he would ever see the light again. He sat on the edge of his seat holding his materials tight. He looked ahead and saw a pinpoint of light. A light was shining at the end of the tunnel. Inside the tunnel was total darkness and for a moment it felt magical and mystical. Bruce saw the light growing brighter as the train pulled through the darkness and entered New York City's Grand Central Station.

He could feel the train slowing down and preparing to stop. "I'm here, I'm really here," Bruce thought to himself.

If he had had a free hand he would have pinched himself but both hands were loaded down with his materials. He knew it was time to leave the train. Bruce carried a briefcase with his *Manifesto* over his shoulder and a two-foot-by-two-foot square cardboard box tied with a thick, wooly cord for his carefully constructed model. He also carried a precisely bound roll of blueprints under his arm that his Dad had copied for him. They were printed from the ink drawings he had diligently prepared in his mechanical drawing class at school.

He felt ready and as he stepped out of the train and looked around Grand Central Station he had a sense of awe and wonder. Standing in the middle of the train terminal he noticed how beautiful it was. Light poured in from huge, high windows and he saw vendors all around the station selling pastries, coffee and newspapers. Everywhere he looked people rushed from one end of the terminal to the other. They pushed, shoved and rushed knowing what they were doing and where they were headed.

For just a moment he was stunned and couldn't move. He asked himself, "What have I done? It's time to get moving. Nothing is going to happen if I keep standing here and staring. I'm ready to fight the fight. Bring it on!"

Looking all around the station he finally saw the exit he wanted. "It will bring me up to street level," he told himself. So, that's where he headed, bumped and shoved every step of the way.

His rolled-up plans were knocked out from under his arm and they fell to the ground. Then his briefcase slid off of his shoulder. He bent down to pick them up before they got trampled. No one offered to help. People could see him struggle to keep everything together but it didn't matter.

"Welcome to New York City," he thought. "No mercy. Everyone looks out for themselves, I guess."

Once he had the plans and everything else organized he continued walking toward the exit. Each step reminded him of the other times he had visited the City with his parents. This time was so different. He was alone and everything seemed bigger than life. Traffic noise was louder than he remembered and he found that all of his senses were on overload. He stopped and thought to himself, "Well, I'm finally here. What's next?"

As he stood by himself coming up the stairs to street level he stopped again for a moment and looked both ways, deciding which way to go. The heat and humidity were merciless and slammed him with full force. It was June and hot—ninety degrees with what seemed like one hundred percent humidity and it was only eight o'clock in the morning. The day was just starting.

Self-doubt and fear began to rear their ugly heads as he stood on the sidewalk and was shoved back and forth by people rushing to get to work. He felt invisible. It was as if no one saw him. When someone bumped into him no one apologized either. "How can they not see me with all of my stuff? I'm no ninety-eight-pound weakling."

Realizing he could do nothing about it he stepped into the flow of humanity and moved forward. "This is what being in a rapidly moving river must feel like only this is a rapidly moving river of humanity. Welcome to morning rush hour in New York City," he thought.

Bruce kept walking with no destination in mind, going with the flow of people traffic. It was easier than going against the flow. "So what if everyone here is rude and won't talk to me. I've got a mission to accomplish and I'm going to finish it," he exclaimed.

He had a general idea where he was headed: toward Fifth Avenue on what appeared to be Forty-Second Street. He kept asking himself, "What am I doing? Where am I going? Okay, what's next? What do I do now?"

Having made a random choice of direction, all of a sudden he saw two lions guarding some steps ahead of him. He felt this was his destination and reasoned, "Of course, there it is! I'm headed to The New York Public Library. It's the best library in the world! I will make this my beachhead. It will be my home base and I can work from here."

Feeling more confident a determined Bruce headed straight for the library. As he walked up the steps he juggled his cargo and was impressed with how large the library appeared to be. It was majestic, grand and elegant. He entered through the huge glass doors and felt a sense of silence and reverence immediately. "You can almost hear a pin drop. I feel safe and secure," he thought as he felt the silence and peace of the library surround him.

Libraries were no strangers to Bruce. He found solace in his high school library as he recovered from his football injury. The calm and quiet atmosphere of Drew University's library provided what he needed to research, create and refine his *Manifesto* which led to the Astronarium and Science Center. It seemed natural that the next phase of his project would be created within the halls of yet another library. "Man, this is some library," he marveled.

"I've hit the jackpot and this is like a palatial oasis in the middle of madness. It feels safe, quiet, and warm. It will give me a chance to gather my thoughts and do my research. All of my senses feel as though they are overloaded right now. This is where I can prepare for battle!"

He looked around and noticed that far more information was stored in this library than the others. He was excited to begin his research. For the next five days he used the resources of The New York City Library to identify people, decision-makers and large companies to contact. Then he would arrange appointments with key people so he could present his Astronarium and Science Center proposal to them.

As he evaluated and analyzed his research he chose to focus on companies that would have an interest in and be drawn to technology. He narrowed his search and zeroed in on high tech, engineering, oil and defense companies. Bruce felt as if he had hit the jackpot. New York City was the home of many major corporations that stretched throughout the world.

Next he identified key decision-makers within these companies and gathered as much information about them as possible. He searched newspaper clippings, corporate annual reports, and anything else that was written about the people he wanted to see. Bruce thought this must be like mining for gold.

By the end of the week he had accumulated a formidable list of who's who in New York City's Fortune 500 companies. He had names and addresses of the companies and who the decision-makers were. "I'm ready to leave the library now. My research is done and I'm ready to hit the streets. I have everything that I need with me. I'm glad that the train station has lockers where I can keep my materials overnight."

KNOCKING ON DOORS

Full of optimism Bruce hit the streets and began to pound the pavement during his second week in New York. His spirits were at an all-time high and he felt ready to meet with the power brokers of New York! Every day he contacted people and companies on his list. Daily he spent at least eight hours outdoors in the heat and humidity while he walked the streets from one place to the next. By the end of the day he was exhausted.

His daily routine was the same. He arrived each morning by train, walked to the next contact on his list, rode the elevators up and down or climbed lots of stairs while carrying his briefcase, model and materials. Then it was back to the train station and home at night.

This became a repetitive cycle all week. He began to see a trend by the end of the week. "No one will see me! Not one major executive seems interested in what I have to say," thought a discouraged Bruce. "At least I know the best resting places in Midtown Manhattan."

His daily routine included stopping at a few of the resting places when he stopped to eat the bagged lunch that his Mom had prepared and sent with him. He learned to watch people and enjoy observing them while he ate lunch. New York City seemed like a melting pot of humanity to him. People of all sizes, colors and shapes roamed the streets. Bruce found the streets filled with many kinds of characters.

One of his favorite characters was a man he called Moon Dog—a sidewalk musician who wandered around the streets dressed like a Viking wearing a helmet with horns. Another street person was called The Green Giant, a seven-foot tall man with a full beard who dressed all in green like one of Robin Hood's medieval men. He carried a large wooden staff and often stopped right in front of Bruce. He silently stared at the big cardboard box Bruce always carried, the one containing his Astronarium and Science Center model. After he stared at Bruce for a while he would walk away and leave so that Bruce could eat his lunch.

One day while he was eating his lunch something unusual happened. The Green Giant stopped and actually spoke to Bruce. In a slow and deep voice he asked him, "Why do you carry the box?"

Bruce was stunned by this unusual turn of events and took a moment to choose his words carefully: "Because I have to carry the box," he replied.

After several seconds of thoughtful consideration The Green Giant asked, "What is in the box?"

Responding even slower Bruce answered, "All of my dreams!"

Knowingly The Green Giant looked at Bruce and then nodded his head as he quietly walked away.

Another character that Bruce met was a 500-pound pretzel vendor who located his cart at the top of the subway station stairs. It was right at the entrance to the street. "It doesn't matter where I enter or exit, he's always there!" Bruce thought. He seemed to stare and look right at Bruce with his blind and cataract-covered eyes. Bruce thought, "There he is again. This is getting creepy."

Feeling uncomfortable the next thing Bruce heard was a sound that he swore was a bullfrog. He looked all around knowing that frogs weren't inside Grand Central Station. He looked up and there was the pretzel man shouting, "PERETZZELS!" He couldn't believe that the sound came from the pretzel vendor. He quickly looked away and hurried. He couldn't get away fast enough. Then the next thing he heard was what sounded like a sinister, deep laugh, so, he hurried faster. It seemed that the pretzel man had felt Bruce's discomfort and was laughing at him.

Bruce wanted to avoid seeing him again, but it wasn't meant to be. Pretzel man was a regular on the streets. After a while Bruce learned to accept him.

In addition to these colorful characters that he saw daily, Bruce witnessed many homeless people wandering aimlessly on the streets. He believed that they represented the underbelly of New York City. In his sixteen years he had not had any experience with homeless street people.

As he walked down the street and thought about the diversity of people in the City he stopped suddenly. "I can't believe it. There's another character on the streets of New York now and it's me! I'm the boy in the suit with the Big Box! To most people it probably looks like I'm wandering around with no destination, getting asked to leave the best places in the City by the most attractive receptionists!"

As he continued to walk he felt a swell of emotion. "The City is swallowing me up. Does any of this even matter? I've been wandering these streets and trying to see people for days and all I hear is 'NO!' I'm tired. I don't know what to do or how to change it," thought a disheartened Bruce.

That day he felt just like one of the hundreds of nameless street people. "I'm just like one of the reclusive, eccentric and somewhat unstable men and women on the streets who seem to have their own sense of purpose and intention. They appear to be invisible to everyone else, just as I do. It's as though we're from some other planet or living in another dimension. Everyone just ignores us." He continued walking.

He sat down to take a break in Rockefeller Plaza and unpacked the lunch his Mom had made. Feeling down and tired he remembered her advice: "No matter how this all turns out, Bruce, just do your best. In the end you only have to face yourself in the mirror. Did you try your hardest? Did you do your best?"

As he thought about it he gave himself another pep talk: "I haven't come this far to quit! I'm going to continue and see every last person on my contact list even if they all say 'no.' I'm doing my best. I always have and I always will. I'm not a quitter."

Determined, he finished his lunch, threw away the trash and looked across the street. "There's St. Patrick's Cathedral. Just for good measure, I think I will go inside and say a prayer and light a candle for my grandfather. Maybe my Dad was right. Do people really think I'm only a stupid working-class kid from Jersey with nothing of value to say? He can't be right, can he?"

PERSEVERANCE PAYS OFF

Although at times Bruce felt discouraged, he didn't give up. During the third week he diligently continued to follow his plan, contacting the companies and the people on his list every day.

Something needed to change. So, he thought about what he had experienced recently. "Okay, it's Wednesday and all I have heard this week is 'NO!' 'Do you have an appointment?' 'Mr. So-and-So is out of town' or 'he can't see you today.' 'Didn't you see the sign when you came in—no solicitations?' 'Security, will someone please get Security and remove this person?' I still don't want to give up. I will find a way to get through to these people."

He was discouraged and frustrated. He asked himself, "How do I change these 'NOs' to 'YES'?"

Based on his experience with these big companies and their practices he came to some conclusions. He reviewed them in his mind. "In order to get a job as a receptionist at one of these big companies you have to follow three things:

1) Be very good looking, 2) be quite indifferent and 3) know how to say 'no!'"

After his experiences meeting with at least thirty different receptionists during his contacts he formed his conclusions. All of them seemed to have the same qualities as far as he was concerned. Not one of them appeared to be the least bit interested in who he was or what he had to say. He thought, "They are just gatekeepers. Maybe they're doing what they're supposed to do, but I'm not going to let them stop me."

"Is today going to be like all of the rest?" he wondered as he went over his list.

"Let's see. First stop today is Shell Oil's worldwide headquarters. I want to see the president," a determined Bruce said to himself.

He was dressed for battle. He looked professional and was focused as he made his way to Shell Oil. As he approached the building it seemed huge, a giant monolith with white marble towers. It looked formidable. Two beautiful fountains decorated the front entrance. It was located right on the Avenue of the Americas, a prestigious location.

As he continued to admire the beautiful building he craned his neck upward in order to see the top of the building. He thought, "This place must be important."

He remembered his strategy. "The first step is to get past the receptionist and Security. Then the next step is to meet with Shell Oil US's president."

He walked into the huge lobby area through the massive glass doors and passed Security with no problem. He realized that this was a public lobby and off to the side of the reception area was a bank of elevators that would take a person up to the right floors. "If anyone thinks I look a little strange carrying all of this stuff into the elevator, they aren't saying anything. One down, and now I have to get past the Shell Oil receptionist. No problem," he smiled to himself.

He made it. Another step accomplished. He headed to the bank of elevators carrying all of his materials. He realized his next stop and contact was on the thirty-fifth floor and as he stepped off of the elevator on the thirty-fifth floor he confidently walked up to the Shell Oil receptionist's desk. She was very attractive. "No surprise there," he thought.

"My name is Bruce Tully and I'm here to see the president of Shell Oil on a matter of national security," he quickly explained to the receptionist.

Before he could say anything else she interrupted, sounding very unimpressed and bored. "He's not in and it's doubtful that he will be in today. Do you have an appointment?"

"Oh, not this again," he thought. "Another 'NO' is coming."

At that very moment he heard the elevator door open. Two passengers stepped off. One was a very large black man wearing sunglasses who got out first. He was followed by a very dignified older man wearing what looked to be a very expensive suit. He came over to the receptionist and said, "Good morning."

She responded very quickly and politely, "Good morning, Dr. Spaght. I hope you had a very nice trip into the City this morning."

Bruce stood there totally shocked and amazed. "Dr. Spaght? He's the president of Shell Oil US and he's on my list. He's the person I want to see. Now what do I do?" he asked himself.

Before he could organize his thoughts and recover from his surprise both men disappeared behind a locked door. "Now what?" he wondered.

He recovered and thought to himself, "I was standing only a foot away from the president of Shell Oil US, the person I want to see."

So he turned around and went back to the receptionist and said, "I just saw him arrive. I want you to announce me. Tell him I'm here to see him. I know he will want to see me. Come on, he looks like a good guy. He will see me."

Clearly she didn't feel the same way. She sneered and replied, "Not a chance, kid. I get paid to keep people like you away from people like him. If you don't leave right now, I'm going to call Security."

"Okay! Okay! I'm leaving." He thought, "I don't want to get thrown out. What am I doing wrong?" He backed up towards the elevators wanting to avoid a confrontation.

Even though he was told "NO" Bruce still felt a sense of accomplishment. "I actually saw him and heard the man speak. He's real. It's more than I can say for the others on my list. Man, I'm going to see this guy, no matter what. Hey, now I know what he looks like!"

For the next few days Bruce felt like a spy. He returned to the Shell Oil offices and was determined to find a way to meet Dr. Spaght, the president of this prestigious and powerful American company. He hoped he would see him again. While he watched the comings and goings of people he noticed when Dr. Spaght arrived for work. "He's very punctual and seems to follow a routine. He arrives between 9:00 a.m. and 9:15 a.m. every morning," observed Bruce.

A plan began to form in his mind. Bruce decided that the best way to get in to see Dr. Spaght was to sneak past the Security people in the lobby and climb the emergency stairs that normally were only used in case of fire. "I can carry my presentation materials to the thirty-fifth floor Executive Suites where I originally saw Dr. Spaght," he thought.

"When I reach the door I will leave it cracked open a little and watch to see who comes and goes. I can see when he gets out of his private elevator. Then I will step through the door and approach him."

It sounded simple and easy. He knew that timing was critical. "If I step out too early, the receptionist will call Security and have me escorted out of the building. I don't have a better plan right now," thought Bruce. "I'm going to try it tomorrow."

With a workable plan he felt good. "I can't wait to get into the City tomorrow. I know I'm in good shape and can tackle the thirty-five floors of stairs with no problem," he thought confidently. "I'm an athlete and I am still in great shape."

He continued to think more about his plan as he listened to the sounds of the train on the ride into the City the next morning. He had taken extra care dressing and felt totally prepared. "I wonder if there's another way to reach my goal. I can't think of anything else and I have to see Dr. Spaght, the president of Shell Oil US! This has got to work."

As he continued to think about his plan he tried to anticipate several outcomes. It seemed as though a million thoughts raced through his mind all at the same time: "What will I do if I see him? What if I get tossed out? What if I get thrown in jail?"

Before he knew it the train arrived at Grand Central Station. This morning was no different than any other morning. His senses were heightened and he was on alert. He heard all of the sounds around him. The scents from the bakeries were wonderful in the train station. Yet as he exited to street level the local characters seemed less important. He was focused on his mission and he had no room for distractions.

Bruce collected his presentation materials from the train station locker and headed out to the Shell offices. He arrived early and knew it would take him at least thirty minutes to climb the stairs to the thirty-fifth floor. "Juggling and balancing all of my stuff will slow me down some. I have time," thought Bruce. "I need a distraction so I can get through the lobby and by Security unnoticed. What can I do?"

He remembered meeting a street group of mime performers earlier in the week while he ate lunch in front of the Shell Oil building. "If I see the mime, I will ask him if he will do a small performance in the public lobby. He will create a perfect distraction and I will pay him five dollars to do it."

Bruce saw the mime was in front of the building as he approached the entrance. He quickly drew the young man away from the group and explained to him what he needed. The mime agreed! On Bruce's signal the mime entered the lobby and went straight to the guard station. He began to do what mimes do, lots of action and no talking. He was moving around and annoying the security guards. "This is perfect," Bruce thought.

The mime's antics gave Bruce the time he needed to slip past the guards unnoticed and reach the stairwell. This was amazing considering all of the stuff he carried with him. He was in! Now for the long climb to the thirty-fifth floor. He was excited!

Soon Bruce was elated. He was soaking wet with sweat and winded as he stood on the thirty-fifth floor stairwell landing, just as he had planned. Slowly he cracked the door open so he could see into the lobby area of the Executive Suites. He heard the receptionist who was at her desk talking and answering the phones. She sounded like a broken record repeatedly saying, "Good morning. Shell Oil. May I help you?"

He was afraid to breathe. "I don't want to get caught and thrown out. I'm so close to my goal of meeting the president of Shell Oil, Dr. Monroe E. Spaght," he thought as he watched people come and go through the cracked-open door.

Suddenly the moment he was waiting for came. The private elevator door opened. He held his breath. "Yes, it's him!" he excitedly told himself.

He immediately threw open the stairwell door and rushed out! "I probably look like a crazy person," he thought. "I'm so excited to meet the president of Shell Oil in person, finally."

Before he reached him, however, he was stopped by the second man who also got out of the elevator, a bodyguard! The next thing he knew the bodyguard grabbed his shoulder and stepped in front of Dr. Spaght, protecting him. Bruce couldn't stop now, "Sir, my name is Bruce Tully and I'm sixteen years old. I've been waiting for days to see you. Please see me, sir. It's a matter of national security."

This distinguished and conservative corporate executive seemed startled and perplexed by Bruce's heartfelt pleas. He didn't know what to make of this kid juggling so many things in his arms and trying to get his attention. "Is this true?" he asked his receptionist "Has he been waiting for days to see me?"

Bruce held his breath while the bodyguard continued to hold onto his shoulder with a firm grip. The receptionist, caught off guard, answered, "Well, yes, sir, he has been coming around. I told him that you were unavailable."

Dr. Spaght didn't hesitate. He turned to his bodyguard and said, "Show this young man into my private conference room and have him wait for me there."

"Yes, sir," replied the bodyguard respectfully as he removed his hand from Bruce's shoulder.

Dr. Spaght turned his attention to Bruce and asked, "Young man, what did you say your name was again?"

"Bruce Tully, sir," he breathlessly replied.

"Well, Bruce, if you have the time to wait, I can see you in about a half an hour. I have a few things to do first," explained Dr. Spaght.

He couldn't believe his luck and what Dr. Spaght said. With enthusiastic relief Bruce responded, "I have all day to wait if that's what you need."

"That's fine, Bruce. All I need is thirty minutes," offered Dr. Spaght.

Dr. Spaght's bodyguard took Bruce to the executive conference room to wait until Dr. Spaght was available. He still couldn't believe his good fortune and was in a state of shock. "This is my chance. I can't believe it's really going to happen. I've been working on this for a year. I can't blow it."

As he waited for Dr. Spaght he took the time to rehearse his presentation, organizing what he was going to say. For just a minute Bruce was afraid. "What am I going to say? I've never made a presentation in my life to anyone. Let's see. I've watched my Dad who's a great speaker and I've been in some school plays. I have even starred in some plays and

I know acting techniques that are used in the theater. I will treat this like a one-act play," he decided.

He composed himself and took a few deep breaths and focused on the positive: "It's finally going to happen!"

He was nervous as he opened his box and laid out his model. He unrolled the set of plans that he designed and drew. At last he pulled out a copy of his *Manifesto* for this powerful corporate executive. "Here I am, nervous, but ready! In a matter of minutes I will be all alone with one of the most powerful men in the country," he imagined. "I can't blow this chance."

He looked around the conference room while he waited, taking in all of the details. On the walls he noticed framed photographs of this powerful man with presidents, senators and other influential people. Bruce did his best not to feel intimidated. "Who do I think I am? Why should he listen to me?" he wondered.

Just then the door opened and the president of Shell Oil US sat down directly across from Bruce. "Now, tell me, Bruce, exactly what is this matter of great national security you have waited all week to see me about?"

He took another deep breath, reached for composure, and then proceeded slowly and with care to explain step by step why he was there. He started from the beginning. He related everything that had transpired over the past year including the Soviet challenge and the conclusions he reached. He presented his *Manifesto* and concluded with a description of the architectural model and the design drawings.

Dr. Spaght listened to the presentation carefully. He was respectful and appeared to be interested. Bruce was encouraged and by the time he was finished an hour had gone by. Dr. Spaght spoke, "My religion teaches that from time to time a generation will hear the words of a 'truth speaker.' After hearing you speak to me today, son, I believe you may be a truth speaker for your generation. You are absolutely right in everything that you have said today. What help do you need from me, Bruce?"

It took a moment for Bruce to recover. He was stunned and couldn't believe what he had just heard. He took a moment to collect his thoughts before he responded. Then he said, "Sir, it's my hope that by seeing you today, a great corporation like Shell Oil can find a way to help me get this need that I have identified fulfilled."

"I will help you, Bruce. A good friend of mine owns one of the largest engineering companies in New York City and does quite a bit of work for me. I would like for you to see him and tell him exactly what you have told me," explained Dr. Spaght.

"I can't believe it. My mission is real. It's going to happen!" Bruce thought as he watched the president of Shell Oil pick up the phone and call his friend immediately.

He listened to Dr. Spaght's telephone conversation: "Hi, Ted, I have a young man sitting with me and he's in my office right now. I have just heard his most extraordinary story and I want you to hear what he has to say. Then I want you to help him! Yes, he's sitting here right now. Okay, I will put him in my car and send him right over if you can see him. Good! I will send him right down."

As Dr. Spaght hung up the phone he turned to Bruce and said, "Ted will see you this morning. I'm going to send you over to his office in my limo. Make sure you tell him everything that you have told me, exactly as you have told me. Don't leave anything out. Oh, yes, one more thing—thank you for seeing me today."

Then he called the receptionist into the conference room and said, "See to it that my driver takes Mr. Tully over to Ted Kauffeld's office. Please do it immediately."

She looked at Bruce and her face showed surprise and shock, "Yes, sir," she replied and left to make the necessary arrangements.

NEXT STEP— THE ENGINEERS

Bruce packed up all of his materials and left the Executive Offices. He took a seat across from the receptionist and waited in the lobby for the driver and the car to arrive. He noticed that the receptionist seemed uncomfortable, maybe even embarrassed for the way she had treated him during his earlier visit. He closed his eyes and savored his victory and thought, "Not only did Dr. Spaght open the door to the next step of my mission. I feel as though I have experienced a moment of triumph over all of the gatekeepers in New York City!"

As he waited he reviewed his meeting and the interaction with Dr. Spaght. "Holy smokes! Wow! I got to see Dr. Spaght. I got to see him! I'm going to ride in a limo and be driven to see another big shot!" All of the frustration, threats and aggravation he had experienced no longer mattered.

He was excited, energized and prepared for his next presentation as the limo pulled up and Dr. Spaght's driver opened the car door for him, waiting until he got inside. Bruce got in and settled down in the back seat with all of his materials and thought as the limo pulled away from the curb, "This is unreal. I'm actually riding in a limousine. I've never been in one before. I can't believe it."

He sat back and enjoyed the air-conditioned ride thinking, "This sure beats walking with the box and all of my presentation materials in the summer heat. Wait until I tell Mom and Dad tonight. My friends won't believe this. No one is going to believe me!"

As he was driven to his next meeting in comfort he watched the buildings and people go by. The limo ride was fast and before he realized it the driver pulled up in front of a classical, turn-of-the century, New York mid-rise building. The driver leaned over, pointed and said, "This is where you get off, kid. Just go in that door right there. The elevator guy will tell you where to go from there."

As Bruce left the comfort of the limo he replied, "Hey, thanks, man! Please thank your boss when you see him again."

"Yeah, yeah, I will," responded the driver as he pulled out into the busy traffic of lower Broadway.

Bruce noticed that he wasn't in Midtown Manhattan anymore. He was well outside of the boundaries that his Dad had carefully defined for him on his dog-eared and well-worn map. He took another minute to get his bearings and looked around. "I must be in lower Manhattan and the financial district," he speculated. "Everything looks different and seems older."

Gone were the tall glass and stone towers of Midtown and in their places were buildings of old New York. From where Bruce stood he could see Trinity Church and Wall Street. Glancing one more time at the building he was entering on Broadway he took a deep breath and entered through the revolving door. He walked confidently across the lobby with all of his materials in his arms and saw the elevator. As he approached it he met an elevator operator in full uniform, reminiscent of old New York. "Where do you want to go, kid?" he asked Bruce.

"I'm here to see Mr. Ted Kauffeld," replied Bruce in his most adult-sounding voice.

"You will want to go to the twelfth floor," the operator said.

Bruce shook his head knowingly.

"Hey, kid, do you know Mr. Kauffeld?" the operator asked on the ride up.

"No," he responded.

"So, kid, is this your first time with him?" the operator asked, filled with curiosity.

Bruce shook his head, "Yes."

"Watch out then, kid. He's tough and doesn't suffer fools very well," said the operator as the elevator abruptly stopped. "This is your stop. Go down the hall to the right. The name is on the door. You can't miss it. Have fun, kid."

The elevator door closed and headed back down to the lobby with its ancient driver at the controls. Bruce walked down a long and silent corridor. He noticed every detail. The walls were ornately carved wood paneling and a thick, rich Oriental rug was on the floor. At the end of the hall he saw two large double doors. Inscribed in very large gold letters was Theodore J. Kauffeld, ME, PE, and the Devenco Companies.

He stood there for a few moments. He was nervous and apprehensive and felt as if butterflies were flying around in his stomach. He thought, "What am I doing here? This is the major leagues. Look at all of this. It's impressive. I haven't felt like this since I broke my leg. Okay, Bruce, it's game time. I wonder what I'm getting myself into."

At last he reached for the doors, pulled them open and walked through before he talked himself out of it. As he entered the reception area he stopped and thought, "Oh, no, not another one of New York's gatekeepers."

The woman sitting behind the desk was different. She was slender, tall and blonde, dressed all in black with her hair pulled severely into a tight bun at the base of her neck. She looked formidable. "How can I help you?" she asked speaking in a soft and condescending voice filled with authority. "My name is Miss Shettie."

"I'm here to see Mr. Kauffeld," answered Bruce.

Tilting her head down she looked at Bruce over the top of her glasses and asked, "And what is your name?"

He replied respectfully, "Bruce A. Tully."

"I don't seem to have you down for an appointment, Mr. Tully. Could there be some mistake?" she asked.

He took a deep breath and thought, "Oh, no, not again." He blurted out, "Miss Shettie, I'm the gentleman Dr. Spaght called Mr. Kauffeld about earlier this morning!"

Relaxing, Miss Shettie said, "Oh, yes, yes, of course. Please come with me."

She stood up and immediately escorted Bruce to a large paneled conference room. "Why don't you sit down, Bruce? Would you like something to drink?"

A nervous Bruce said, "Yes, please. A large glass of water would be nice."

Bruce was impressed as he looked around the conference room taking it all in after Miss Shettie left the room. The walls were paneled with rich, warm wood. He heard a large, ornate grandfather clock ticking in the quiet room. The carpet was so thick and plush that the room seemed soundproof. He turned and looked at what appeared to be the head of the conference table and noticed a huge portrait of a dignified-looking man who held a pair of eyeglasses. "That must be Mr. Kauffeld," he thought.

Suddenly the door swung open and a tall and somewhat portly gentleman walked briskly into the conference room. Bruce was struck by his commanding presence. His appearance was impeccable. He wore a stiff, white as snow, starched shirt, blue and red bow tie, blue blazer and gray slacks. "People dressed like this are usually on television and the actors are impersonating wealthy men," he thought.

Still sitting down Bruce tried not to stare or feel intimidated. Mr. Kauffeld walked toward him and Bruce quickly got out of his chair, standing up and at attention. They shook hands and Mr. Kauffeld was the first one to speak. His face registered surprise. He didn't expect him to be so young. "Now tell me, is it Bruce? What could be so important that Spaght believed he needed to interrupt my morning?"

The words of advice from the elevator operator surfaced so Bruce got straight to the point. "It's a matter of national security, sir!"

Mr. Kauffeld leaned over and looked Bruce in the eye. He asked with some skepticism, "Oh, really, a matter of great national importance? What do you know about that?"

"I've been working for about a year on my project. The Assistant Superintendent of Schools thought it was important and he directed the Principal of my high school to let me work on it during class. After Dr. Spaght heard my presentation and story today he called me a "truth speaker" for my generation. Then he picked up the phone and called you and thought you needed to hear every word of my presentation," explained Bruce.

Interrupting Bruce's story Mr. Kauffeld said, "Fine, young man, I know that! That's why you're here. What exactly do you have to say?"

Bruce felt intimidated. He had never met anyone like this before. He felt like a fish out of water so he remained quiet and thought to himself. "This is a whole new experience. Now what do I do?"

Kauffeld quickly moved on: "How old are you anyway?"

"I'm sixteen, sir," replied Bruce quickly.

"Well, then, let's hear what you have to say" he said and quickly picked up the phone. He spoke to his secretary: "I'm not to be disturbed."

Bruce watched Mr. Kauffeld fold his arms across his chest and then sit back, making himself comfortable in his large, leather swivel chair. Then he turned to Bruce and said, "Please proceed."

"It's now or never," Bruce thought as he prepared to deliver his presentation to this formidable man.

He launched into the presentation and presented the same material, telling his story exactly as he had two hours earlier, just as Dr. Spaght had told him to do. Nothing was left out. When he was finished he watched the expression on Mr. Kauffeld's face slowly change from indifference to interest. Mr. Kauffeld was fully engaged and interested in what he had to say.

"I'm encouraged," he thought to himself and said, "Well, I'm finished, Mr. Kauffeld. I hope I didn't waste your time this morning, sir. Thank you for listening."

"Waste my time? On the contrary, Bruce. May I call you 'Bruce'? What you've just shared with me is absolutely true. I was discussing this very issue at the University Club with some friends over lunch just the other day. We're all concerned," explained Mr. Kauffeld passionately. "My business depends on the quality of men and women that come out of the universities of tomorrow. We here, at TJK, are worried that people of your generation may not be equipped for the engineering challenges of the future. You have hit the nail on the head, Bruce. Wait here. I want you to talk with my executives right now."

Before Bruce could say anything Mr. Kauffeld got up and left the room. Bruce waited for him to return with his staff.

He was back in less than five minutes. Several men in suits trailed after him. As they entered the conference room and sat down around the table Mr. Kauffeld said to Bruce, "I want you to tell my staff just what you told me. Tell them all of it, every word."

As Bruce looked around the conference table he saw six more impressive men in suits. They ranged in age. Some smoked pipes and others carried yellow note pads and were ready to take notes. He was nervous and thought, "These guys are impressive and kind of intimidating. What will they expect from me? I don't want to disappoint them. I don't have the degrees and experience that they have! I have come this far. I can't quit now. Let's do this!"

All of the men around the table looked as though they were ready to listen, so Bruce began. After repeating his presentation they asked him several questions which he fielded easily. They had questions about design and engineering details. A couple of the men were surprised and voiced disbelief. "Did you really come up with this all by yourself?"

He assured them it was his own and an original project. With their questions answered everyone seemed satisfied. Each of the men stood up, shook Bruce's hand, then turned and left the room leaving Mr. Kauffeld and Bruce alone. Mr. Kauffeld also shook his hand and handed his business card to Bruce. "This is my private home number, Bruce. I want you to call me at this number tomorrow afternoon. I'll be off of the golf course and home from the club by three o'clock.

Make sure you call me, and don't lose this number. It's unlisted!" he directed.

"Yes, sir, Mr. Kauffeld. I will call you tomorrow. Thank you for seeing me today and listening to my presentation about my vision. Thank you for arranging for your staff to hear it too," replied Bruce enthusiastically.

"No problem, Bruce. The pleasure is all ours," responded Mr. Kauffeld as he picked up the phone and said, "Paula, please get George up here. So, where do you live, Bruce?"

"In Madison, New Jersey, sir," answered Bruce.

"Really! That makes us neighbors. I live in Convent Station, the next town over. A Jersey boy, I should have known. You know, I was a Jersey boy once, too many years ago," reflected Kauffeld.

Before long a large middle-aged man dressed in a chauffeur's uniform wearing boots and a black cap appeared at the door. "George, please drive Mr. Tully to the train station so he can take the Lackawanna back to Madison. It's Friday and he will want to get home early," directed Mr. Kauffeld.

"Please come with me, Mr. Tully. I have the car waiting out front," offered George.

Bruce left the office with George and they walked to the elevator. He noticed the elevator operator was the same old guy that delivered him earlier. He looked at Bruce, winked and gave a knowing nod. "Going down," he said.

As they left the main lobby and headed out the front doors Bruce looked up and saw a beautiful, large, black limo parked right in front of the office building. George walked over to it and opened the door for Bruce. "Wow, two limo rides in one day. I could get used to this! Who's going to believe this?"

He was excited on the train ride home. His parents were both home when he arrived and he began to tell them about his exciting day. "We have a lot to celebrate tonight," he explained.

His parents were amazed as he recounted his story. "You met with the president of Shell Oil US?" his mother asked in disbelief.

"They actually listened to you?" his father questioned.

"Yes, they really did, Dad!" Bruce responded with a feeling of accomplishment. "More than that. They called me a 'truth speaker for my generation.'"

"Two limo rides," his mother sighed.

"Yeah, Mom, two!"

Bruce's excitement was contagious and his Dad stood up decreeing, "This family has a lot to celebrate tonight. We're going to Spirito's for dinner! Come on, get in the car!"

Spirito's was Bruce's favorite Italian restaurant and it was located in "Little Italy," a section of Elizabeth, New Jersey. He was excited and joined in the family festivities. "I'm going to have my favorites tonight, Jersey style tomato pie, antipasto, and my favorite dessert, shaved Italian lemon ice. It doesn't get any better than this," he thought to himself. "My Dad is proud of me for once. He hardly ever gives me any praise and I rarely see him smile. I can't remember the last time I've had so much fun with Mom and Dad. I'm glad things finally seem to be going well, and I can't forget to call Mr. Kauffeld tomorrow."

NEXT STEP—THE ENGINEERS 119

A JOB OFFER

Bruce and his family enjoyed their celebration dinner at Spirito's. Although he was excited Bruce slept well that night and at precisely three o'clock the following afternoon he nervously dialed the phone number that Mr. Kauffeld had given to him, his private unlisted number. The phone rang and then it was picked up. "Kauffeld residence. May I help you?" asked a distinctly British-sounding voice.

"Yes. May I speak to Mr. Kauffeld?" Bruce asked.

"Whom shall I say is calling?" asked the distinguished voice.

"This is Mr. Bruce Anthony Tully," answered Bruce throwing in his middle name, Anthony, to match the formal tone of the conversation.

"Mr. Kauffeld asked me to call him today after three o'clock."

"If you will kindly wait, I will see if he is available," responded the distinguished-sounding voice.

A few minutes later Mr. Kauffeld was on the phone and said, "Bruce, I'm very glad you called today. I would like for you to come over to my home this afternoon. I have something very important to discuss with you."

"I will see if I can get there. Just a minute, sir."

He covered the mouthpiece and whispered to his Mom who was standing right there, "He wants me to come over to his home right now! What should I tell him, Mom?"

"Tell him 'yes!'" she whispered back.

Bruce told Mr. Kauffeld, "I can come right over. How do I get there? You said that we are neighbors."

Mr. Kauffeld gave Bruce directions to his home. "I live on Punch Bowl Road. Don't worry, Bruce, you can't miss it. I will have George wait out front for you. Look for him."

Bruce thanked him, hung up and then he and his Mom immediately left for the Village of Convent Station, New Jersey. It was a small, exclusive community settled around a turn-of-the-century Roman Catholic convent. In addition to the convent, a beautiful private country club was located in the center of the village and it was surrounded by palatial estates. As they drove through this beautiful area Bruce speculated to himself, "It seems as though only a chosen few can live here."

Bruce realized they were close to Mr. Kauffeld's home. He saw the turnoff and let his Mom know where to turn. She made the turn onto a private road as the instructions indicated. At the end of the private road they noticed two large and impressive stone pillars that marked the entrance to the Kauffeld estate. They continued driving. As they drove between the two pillars they entered a tree-lined drive. They were immediately surrounded by a canopy formed by the trees. The covered drive seemed to go on forever. Then, as if appearing straight out of a fairytale, there loomed in front of them a large, stone, medieval-looking castle-like mansion complete with turrets.

As Mr. Kauffeld promised, George, the chauffeur was there, patiently waiting and dressed in full uniform. Bruce got out of the car. He turned back to say "good-bye" to his Mom and she said, "I will be back for you in an hour. Please be out front."

"Thanks, Mom," Bruce responded dutifully.

George walked toward Bruce and spoke, "It's nice to see you again, Mr. Tully. I will show you to the door."

As they walked toward the door a butler appeared and was dressed in full morning coat, complete with cravat and spats. "My name is William," he said. "I will show you to the drawing room. Please follow me."

Bruce was amazed as he noticed his surroundings and followed the butler down the hall. The interior of the mansion was cavernous. It looked like a museum complete with suits of armor. Tapestries adorned the walls and what appeared to be Renaissance Old Masters' paintings hung everywhere he looked. "Man, what am I doing here? I'm way out of my league," he thought.

He was shown into the drawing room and as he looked around he noticed heavy, wood paneling and a coffered ceiling. The room felt warm, rich and intimidating at the same time. All of the side tables had cut crystal and silver on them. "This is nothing like my house," he thought.

"Please have a seat," offered William as he pointed Bruce to a large, dark, ornately carved wood partners' desk, "Would you like some sherry?"

"No, thank you," responded Bruce politely.

"Would you like a cup of tea?" asked William.

"That would be great. Thank you," answered Bruce.

William left the room, having made sure that Bruce was comfortable, and promptly returned with a silver tray filled with a plate of small pastries and a pot of tea. "This is amazing," thought Bruce.

"I hope this will meet with your satisfaction," said William.

"Thank you very much, William. This is great," responded Bruce.

Reassured that Bruce was comfortable, William turned around and left the room. Bruce was alone. The room was so quiet that the only thing he heard was the ticking of a large captain's clock over the fireplace. Looking all around and taking in these plush surroundings he thought, "This must be how it feels to sit in a European castle built for royalty. I have never seen anything so grand. The closest thing to this is the Cloister Museum in New York City. My parents took me there several years ago. I can't believe this mansion is so close to the tract house I live in. I feel as if I'm on another planet."

He was nervous and continued to wait for Mr. Kauffeld. As the clock struck four bells the large double doors opened and there stood Mr. Theodore J. Kauffeld, the master of the manor house. He looked the part. He was dressed in a smart Black Watch plaid jacket with black silk lapels, black slacks and black leather slip-on shoes with tassels. Bruce noticed that underneath his jacket he wore a heavily starched white button-down collared shirt that was unbuttoned at the collar. "Even at home he dresses formally."

He walked over and joined Bruce at the desk. He asked, "Do you mind if I smoke?"

"No, not at all, Mr. Kauffeld," Bruce answered.

Bruce watched as he removed a long and probably very expensive cigar or what Bruce imagined as a hand-rolled Cuban cigar. The cigar was stored in a humidor behind the desk. As Bruce watched Mr. Kauffeld it seemed as though he was performing some kind of ritual. He watched him clip the end of the cigar precisely before it was lit. Then he took a long draw from the cigar and offered to Bruce, "I have these imported directly from my source in Havana. Would you like to try one?"

Bruce was surprised at the offer and said, "No, no, thank you, sir. Thank you for offering anyway."

He continued to watch Mr. Kauffeld take another long and what looked to be a very pleasurable draw on his cigar. Then Mr. Kauffeld gently placed the cigar in a very large, cut-crystal ashtray on the desk. He was ready to take care of business.

He turned back to Bruce and said, "Let me tell you why I've asked you here today. After you left my office yesterday my executive staff and I discussed you and your project at great length. We were very impressed with you, your story, and the work you have done."

Bruce sat up straighter as he listened to what Mr. Kauffeld told him. He was pleased with what he heard. "I don't want to miss a single word," he thought.

Kauffeld continued to speak. "Because of this we have decided to help you accomplish your objectives with your Astronarium and Science Center. The full resources of our office staff will be at your disposal. They will focus on helping you in any way they can. We agree that your project is greatly needed by the young people of the United States of America. I, personally, am committed to see that this gets built."

Bruce leaned back in his chair. He was in shock as he remembered his journey. "This is unreal. Only two days ago I was dragging myself, my box, the drawings, my briefcase and lunch from one building to another in Midtown New York. For weeks all I have heard is 'no!'"

He remembered the positive feedback that he received yesterday, first from Dr. Spaght, the president of Shell Oil US, and then from Mr. Kauffeld and his staff. So many thoughts and questions went through his mind at once: "This is really happening. I can't believe it! Am I dreaming? Here I am, in this wild and medieval country estate with one of the most powerful consulting engineers in the country and he's telling me that I'm on target! All of my hard work, late nights, and efforts have finally paid off! He really wants to help me!"

He heard Kauffeld continue with his explanation. "I'm prepared to offer you a summer job at our firm beginning on Monday with a salary of sixty-five dollars a week. You will work exclusively on your project with one of our senior civil and structural engineers. Once we have developed the concept a little more we will retain one of the best architectural firms in the City to help you refine the aesthetic value of your design. I'm considering my friends at La Pierre and Litchfield. Young Larry Litchfield graduated from Cornell's School of Architecture and I think he will be a perfect design partner for you and your project."

Bruce had a hard time keeping up. His head was spinning with possibilities. Everything was happening so fast. It felt as if the floodgates had just opened. He did his best to remain calm and professional but his excitement continued to grow.

"Well, what do you think, Bruce?" he heard Mr. Kauffeld ask.

He was so excited that his heart was pounding and he felt as though he might explode. Clearing his throat he managed to say, "I don't know what to say or how to thank you and your staff for believing in me and my vision, Mr. Kauffeld. I accept your offer and I will be honored to work at your firm this summer."

Laughing, Kauffeld stood up, shook Bruce's hand and said, "Welcome to the firm, son. Welcome to the firm. Your parents will have to agree and if it's okay with them, I will see you at the office on Monday at nine o'clock." Then he rang for the butler and asked William to escort Bruce to the front door.

Bruce was excited and his thoughts were still swirling as he walked out of the house. He looked up and saw his Mom patiently waiting for him in the car at the head of the large circular driveway.

He could hardly contain his excitement. Instead of running to tell her the good news he tried to walk quickly but still appear dignified, wanting to get to the car as fast as he could. As he opened the car door and before he was fully inside, his curious Mom couldn't wait any longer to find out what happened. She asked many questions at once! "Well, what happened in there? How did it go? What did he want with you?"

Bruce wondered where to begin so he took a deep breath and said, "Mom, you aren't going to believe it. He told me his executive staff is totally impressed with what I presented and they have agreed to support my project. He said they will do anything they can to see that it gets built! Can you believe it?"

His excitement was contagious and he had to concentrate to keep himself from bouncing off of the front seat. He continued, "That's not all, Mom. He offered me a job with his company for the summer. I begin on Monday morning at nine o'clock and I will be making sixty-five dollars a week working with his staff on my project. I need a permission letter from you to make it official!"

She looked at Bruce and realized the importance of this moment for him. She was so happy and shared his excitement. She couldn't contain herself though and screamed and shouted with joy! He looked at his Mom screaming and then he screamed too. This was one of the happiest moments in his life. After a couple of minutes they settled down. She started the car and they began their journey back home. Bruce continued to watch as the Kauffeld mansion slowly disappeared in the rearview mirror.

CAN WE BUILD IT?

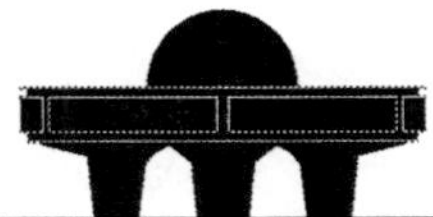

The weekend seemed to fly by. Bruce was nervous and excited about beginning his new job, taking his project to the next level and getting it built. This was a new chapter and he was ready to start working for Theodore J. Kauffeld and Associates in New York City. Monday morning arrived and he was more than ready. Today was different. He had a destination and a job. "No more going door to door and pounding the pavement only to be rejected and told 'NO,'" thought Bruce as he headed in to the office.

He walked through the door at 8:45 a.m., arriving fifteen minutes early. "No way am I going to be late today," he thought to himself. "This time I'm entering this impressive office as the newest member of a nationally respected consulting engineering firm. I'm not sneaking in."

He wore a brand-new navy blue suit, red-and-blue striped tie and a white buttoned-down collared shirt. His other suits were starting to show wear from trudging the streets of Manhattan over the past month and they were at the cleaners. Needless to say, Bruce was thrilled and excited. He couldn't wait to start.

"Well, good morning, Mr. Tully," greeted Miss Shettie. "It's so nice to see you here today."

"Good morning to you too, Miss Shettie. I'm really happy to be here," responded Bruce feeling as if he was at the top of his game and had just won the State football championship.

"Please come with me, Bruce. Mr. Kauffeld will be in shortly and I know he will want to see you first thing," directed Miss Shettie as she took him to a guest office to wait.

Bruce speculated, "This feels like the calm before the storm," as Miss Shettie left him to wait for Mr. Kauffeld.

Before long Mr. Kauffeld arrived and everything began to happen all at once. First, several key staff members were asked to join in an all-morning brainstorming session. Bruce observed how disciplined the team and its leader were and thought to himself, "They understand what it means to value time. It's how consulting engineers make money. They are treating my project just like any other project here. If time is spent on it, then it's going to be tightly organized."

As the brainstorming session began, Mr. Kauffeld took off his jacket and rolled up his sleeves, clearly ready to begin. "Now let's go over the morning agenda," he said. "By lunch we will have our business plan objectives defined. So, let's get started."

"This is an amazing experience. I'm really part of this highly functioning team of professionals," thought Bruce. "I still feel as if this is a dream."

As the brainstorming and the morning evolved he heard every aspect of his project challenged. The team looked for flaws in the Astronarium concept and all of the work that had been done to date. After each element was thoroughly discussed they moved on to look at various ways to fund construction. Questions were thrown out by the group: "Who can build it? How will it be funded? Who will operate it? Is it self-sustaining?"

Bruce was proud of what was happening and thought, "I'm honored to be a part of this team."

All of these issues were thoroughly discussed and the pros and cons were debated. The session seemed to take on a life all its own. Jim McDermott, TJK vice-president, pointed out that Robert Moses, Director of Planning and Engineering for New York City, had recently announced plans to host the 1964 or 1965 World's Fair. Moses wanted to locate the Fair in the same place where the 1939 World's Fair had been held. Intrigued Mr. Kauffeld said, "Let's talk about this Fair idea a little more."

What happened next became the foundation of the team's implementation strategy. "Theodore J. Kauffeld and Associates will propose that the Astronarium and Science Center be built as the central U.S. exhibit for the upcoming New York City World's Fair to the government of the United States! The proposed theme for the exhibit will focus on U.S. leadership in all fields of science and technology and emphasize our emerging space program," summarized Kauffeld.

Another team member recommended, "Then after the Fair the building will remain and be operated following Bruce's original vision. It can be used as an interactive National Science Center that's dedicated to stimulate the thoughts and minds of American youth while supporting them as future engineers and scientists of America."

The entire team agreed this plan was powerful since the idea for this Center was created, developed and driven by a sixteen-year-old American boy, Bruce Tully.

"This will send a strong and powerful message to other world leaders and the Soviet Union," said Mr. Kauffeld. "Clearly, the youth of our fine country are not weak, stupid or inferior to anyone. We are ready to stand up to the challenge issued by Mr. Khrushchev."

After checking in with the entire team it was decided. Everyone loved the recommendations. Everyone was behind them. Bruce couldn't believe how much was done in such a short time. "It's not even noon yet and we have a six-month plan with a project presentation completion date of January 1, 1961. We're really going to present my plan to the U.S. government!" he thought. "I like the way things are moving. This phase was completed five minutes early. I'm beginning to understand how things operate at TJK."

Before adjourning for lunch, Mr. Kauffeld announced, "Well, gentlemen, I think we have a plan. Now let's get it done. Bruce, will you join me in my office after lunch?"

The conference room quickly emptied and Bruce remained sitting by himself. He revisited everything that he had experienced, observed and felt during the brainstorming session. "What does it all mean?" he kept asking himself, trying to make all of the pieces fit.

Suddenly it all made sense to him. "Now I know why my grandfather spent so many years teaching me," he realized. "I know how he felt and why I reacted so strongly when I saw Premier Khrushchev. I understand why he gave up everything that mattered to him. I did too. All I thought about was fighting back and proving Khrushchev wrong. I feel as if I have just come out of a fog. I gave up my friends, relationships with my coaches, and my summer vacation. It all makes sense. This is my destiny!"

Sixteen-year-old Bruce continued his reflections. "All of my hard work and sacrifice is finally paying off. All of the days of pounding the pavement in New York City trying to find someone who would listen, all the days of hearing so many people tell me 'no'—all of it is worth every minute of time I spent."

This was a significant and defining moment for Bruce. He wondered, "Is this why I'm here? Is this my sole purpose? Am I supposed to be like David who took down Goliath with nothing more than a slingshot? My slingshot is my *Manifesto* and the model for the Astronarium and Science Center. I seem to be alone and ill-equipped for battle, but I'm willing to face my opponent with whatever I have got!"

He continued to think about how far he had come. "Finally I found some very powerful men of industry who are willing to support me and stand up with me. I'm humbled. Never in my wildest dreams did I realize this could happen. I'm so lucky that through a bunch of twists and turns this is really going to happen. I'm responding to Khrushchev's challenge with a powerful answer. We're not weak and I'm living proof," thought Bruce. "My promise to my grandfather is being fulfilled."

As a result of the morning's brainstorming session the significance suddenly registered and he realized, "I symbolize what's possible for America's youth. My mission is now refined and I'm ready to move forward even though I'm not sure where all of this will lead. I guess I will go and grab some lunch before my next meeting."

He was a working man now and didn't have to bring his lunch from home. With a bit of an advance against his first week's salary from his Dad Bruce decided to explore lower Broadway for a good and inexpensive place to eat. "A little fresh air will do me good and give me a chance to clear my head," he reasoned.

Bruce walked out of the building and decided to follow the flow of foot traffic. He ended up at a place called Chuck Full O' Nuts Sandwich Shoppe right across the street from the office. He was hungry and ordered a variety of half sandwiches while he sat at the counter. The restaurant was famous. It was considered to be a New York tradition born during the recession where you could get half a sandwich for a nickel. Prices hadn't changed that much and you could get two halves for a dollar and a coke for a dime. While he waited for his order he thought to himself, "I'm really happy about the outcome of the meeting this morning."

He began to think more about his destiny. "I will be known as the first Cold War Warrior of my generation," and he felt good about it.

As he sat at the counter and continued to eat his mother's words popped up: "Always be careful what you wish for because you just might get it!"

Immediately he remembered his grandfather and how he suffered at the hands of the Communists. "If only he could be here to see what comes next," wished Bruce.

He finished eating the last of his sandwich halves as he looked at the time. "I need to get back to the office. This was a nice break," he thought.

BACK TO BASICS

He entered Mr. Kauffeld's office at one o'clock sharp. "Bruce, I want you to meet someone. I want you to work with him this summer and I know he will be very helpful," announced Mr. Kauffeld.

He reached over and picked up the phone, then used the intercom to his secretary. Bruce heard him say, "Miss Shettie, will you get Mac up here? Tell him that I need to see him."

"Yes, sir, right away," she replied in a very businesslike manner.

Within minutes a short, stocky and disheveled-looking man with a gray beard appeared. Albert MacCabe, or Mac, as he preferred to be called, looked like a stereotypical engineer, the person behind the scenes who didn't usually meet with clients but was counted on to keep things going. His pants were baggy. His shirt was open at the collar with some kind of Scotch plaid tie and he had the knot drawn down and twisted around his neck. His shirt sleeves were rolled up to his elbows and he wore a green eyeshade.

Bruce couldn't help but stare. He was so different from Mr. Kauffeld and the other staff members. He looked nothing like the "suits" that participated in the earlier morning brainstorming session. Bruce thought, "He looks like a cross between Charlie Weaver, a popular TV character, and some British army sergeant major."

Mac was a true Scotsman who came to the United States after World War II. Bruce learned later that Mac had seen plenty of action as a combat engineer for the Scottish Royal Highlands Regiment. He still carried himself as though he wore a uniform. "Good afternoon, Mr. Kauffeld, sir," Mac barked out.

Like a good soldier Mac stood almost at attention, waiting for his orders. "Mac, I want you to meet Mr. Tully. Today is his first day with us and he's working on a very special and high priority project this summer. I will brief you later. I would like for you to take over Mr. Tully's orientation and education, show him how things are done here at TJK. I want him to share an office with you and work at the extra drafting table you have," explained Kauffeld.

Mac looked over at Bruce, glared and wondered, "What's so special about this kid and why am I just finding out about it?"

Bruce felt Mac's scrutiny from the top of his head to the tip of his toes, like an insect under a microscope. Mac was so quiet Bruce felt very uncomfortable. Finally, after what seemed like forever, Mac replied, "Yes, sir, Mr. Kauffeld. As you wish, sir."

Sensing Bruce's discomfort, Mr. Kauffeld turned to him and said, "You are in very good hands with Mac." Then he turned and left for his next meeting leaving Bruce and Mac alone.

They stood there looking at each other for what seemed like an eternity. Sizing each other up, Mac broke the silence and scornfully said, "Pick up all of your stuff and come with me, Tully. Tully, is it? No doubt you are Irish!"

Mac quickly turned around and began walking away. He expected Bruce to catch up and not lag behind. They traveled out the main office door, down a long hallway, past the elevators and then stopped in front of another small door at the end of the hall. It was marked "Staff Only."

Mac opened the door and they entered another part of the offices. It seemed as though they walked forever and as they continued walking Bruce thought, "We must be entering the bowels of the firm. This is really different from Mr. Kauffeld's offices."

Everywhere he looked he saw people of all ages, colors and ethnic origin. They were engineers and draftsmen sitting in what looked like a sea of cubes. These workstations he noticed were equipped with the best top-of-the-line drafting tables and equipment. Finally, Mac and Bruce reached a small windowless office in the back. This was Mac's domain, Chief Production Engineer and Clerk of the Works.

"Put your stuff down over there. Hang up your jacket on this hanger. You won't need it back here, boy. Now sit down," ordered Mac.

Bruce wondered, "What have I gotten myself into? Is this going to be my torture chamber for the next four months?"

"How old are you anyway," asked Mac.

Bruce felt uncomfortable and quickly replied, "I'm sixteen, sir."

"Save the 'sir' for Kauffeld. I'm Mr. MacCabe to you, boy," directed Mac.

Not one to be easily intimidated, learning from his Dad, Bruce thought to himself, "I can take whatever he dishes out, no matter what. This is nothing."

"It's not like I have spare time around here," Mac roared. "Now the old man has gone and made me a babysitter!"

Hearing this outburst directed at him Bruce winced. "We're not off to a very good start," he thought. "I'm not here to be babysat!"

Rather than be intimidated Bruce decided to see if he could talk to Mac. "Do you want to hear my story?"

"No, be quiet," interrupted Mac. "I'm sure I will hear all about it from the old man later. I don't have time to waste, boy. I will ask the questions and you will give me answers. You got that, boy?"

Bruce was stunned for a minute. Mac was shooting orders in rapid fire order. "Yes, sir. I mean, yes, Mr. MacCabe," answered Bruce.

Mac reminded Bruce of a tyrant. Instead of a Russian one like his father he faced one from Scotland now. "Just call me Mac, boy. It will save us all some time," he shot back.

"Wow," thought Bruce, "a breakthrough. I will take anything right now. I don't care how small it is. Maybe it won't be so bad after all."

Just as he thought things were improving Mac continued to shoot rapid-fire questions: "All right, what engineering school are you in?"

"None, Mac," Bruce replied.

"Well, then, what courses, technical school courses, have you taken? Have you taken calculus, structures, materials or mechanical drawing?" continued Mac.

"I haven't had any of those courses either," responded Bruce.

"What? Well, boy, why not?" asked Mac sounding totally confused.

Looking directly at an unhappy Mac was hard but Bruce tried to make him understand as quickly as he could. "I'm not in technical school. I just finished my junior year at Madison High School. They don't teach those classes there. Mr. Terrell let me sit in on his mechanical drawing class and I drew a set of plans for my project," explained Bruce.

"What in the world are you doing here?" asked a bewildered Mac. "This is a serious engineering firm. It is not a playground!"

Waiting just a minute and deep in thought Mac said, "All right. Maybe you better show me what you think you have in that box. Let me see the drawings too."

Now was his chance to let Mac know why he was here. Bruce quickly laid the drawings out, spreading them flat on the drafting table. Then he took the model for the Astronarium and Science Center out of the box and set it up. When he was done he turned around looking right at Mac and said, "Here it is!"

Bruce thought Mac would understand right away why he was there once he saw his model and drawings. He was proud of his work and felt sure that Mac would think it was really good.

Nothing was said for what seemed like forever. Mac stepped over to the table to see what Bruce had laid out. He was curious. He began to inspect everything—the drawings and the model at the same time. Bruce felt as if he was looking at a ping pong game as Mac's head turned back and forth from drawings to model until he was done. Then Mac stepped away from the table. Bruce said, "It's my Astronarium and Science Center. What do you think?"

He expected praise from Mac but he received the opposite reaction much to his surprise. Mac shouted, "I don't care what it is! There is no way this can be built in one hundred years! Your design defies all sound principles of physics and engineering. It is pie in the sky, boy. You ought to be working at Marvel comics and not here. That's what I think."

Bruce was stunned. This definitely wasn't the response he had expected. "At least he's being honest," he thought.

"Now put those things back in the box. We won't need them again this summer," Mac calmly told Bruce.

"Man, I don't know what I'm going to do now. I thought we were going to work on my project. This is definitely different than the meeting this morning. I guess I'm going to have to follow orders for now," reasoned a bewildered Bruce as Mac stepped out of the room for a few minutes.

He packed up his materials and took them over to the corner of the room. He made sure they were out of the way.

As he finished straightening things up Mac returned with a long narrow box in his hands. "This is a Mayline. The drafting table needs one. Open it up and install it on the table. The directions are in the box and the tools are over there. See if you can handle this since you're so smart. I have work to do and I will be back in an hour," ordered Mac.

He watched Mac turn around again and leave the room.

He picked up the box from the drafting table and realized that a Mayline was a state-of-the-art parallel bar used for drafting. It had recently replaced the old T-square. He thought, "Wow, this is one of the tools that I couldn't afford to buy when I did my project drawings."

Bruce diligently read the assembly directions and began putting the Mayline together. He had almost finished when the door opened and there stood Mac asking, "You done with the Mayline yet?"

"Yes, I am," replied Bruce.

"Good. Let me see it," ordered Mac.

Mac was thorough and inspected every inch of the assembled Mayline while Bruce held his breath. After a thorough review and test Mac proclaimed loudly, "There might be hope for you yet, boy."

He quietly accepted the backhanded compliment as Mac took out a sheet of production grade drafting paper from a large drawer in the table. He watched Mac place it on the table and then square it up with the sliding Mayline. It was like watching a ritual. After the paper was squared up, the opposite corners were stretched and taped with drafting tape securing them snugly to the table. "Did you see how I did that, boy? Now you do the other corners," he directed.

Following Mac's directions exactly, Bruce secured the other two corners. The drafting paper fit snugly on the table and was ready for use. It was so tight there were no creases, folds or looseness.

"You learned something new today. Now that's how I want you to prepare a drafting sheet always before you begin to work on it," directed Mac.

Next he took out a small can of dust and shook it all over the paper. "That's what we call erasure powder. It lets the Mayline ride just above the paper. This way it won't smudge your lines," explained Mac.

As he watched Mac Bruce thought, "He looks like a surgeon. He's so precise and he seems so proud of what he's doing."

Mac reached over and turned on a light that brightened the whole work space. "This takes all of the shadows away when you're working on the drafting table. You can see exactly what you're doing," he instructed.

"Now that the table, paper and tools are ready to go it's time to go to work," Mac went on. "I want you to draft the upper and lower case letters of the alphabet. Then I want you to draft the numbers zero through nine."

Bruce looked at Mac and then quickly did as he was instructed. "Just as I thought," exclaimed Mac, "That mess looks like a dog's dinner. Here, give me the pencil."

Taking the pencil from Bruce, Mac quickly drew three very lightly drawn lines that were guides for printing letters and numbers. He proceeded to produce the most beautiful lettering and numbers that Bruce had ever seen. "See here, that's how you do it," explained Mac. "Now you do it."

Very carefully Bruce tried to copy what Mac had done but to no avail. "It's not that easy, is it, boy? I want you to sit here at the table until you can copy my letters exactly as I have shown you. You are not to leave until I tell you that you are done. I don't care how long it takes. It might be hours, days or weeks as far as I'm concerned. Whether you can do this or not is entirely up to you. You are not allowed to draw one line in this office until you have mastered this. The mark of a good draftsman is the sign of his good lettering."

Bruce made himself comfortable and with focused determination he began to draft letters. It took him the re- mainder of the day and three more days before Mac felt he had passable lettering.

On the fourth day of his employment Mac gave Bruce permission to begin the next step—learning to draw lines! "I'm on a roll," he thought.

During the entire first week of employment Bruce learned how to draw letters and lines. It was late Friday afternoon and he wondered, "What am I doing here? What about my project? How will I get it to the next step?"

Deep in thought and focused on the paper in front of him Bruce was startled when Mac approached him and offered, "Here, take these books home with you tonight and bring them back to work with you on Monday. They were my boy's textbooks from the Academy. He graduated from the Merchant Marine Academy this spring in engineering. He won't need them anymore. Everything you're going to need to know to turn that cartoon of yours into a buildable project is in here."

He handed Bruce a large stack of books that covered a wide range of subjects. "Wow! Thank you, Mac," a happy and surprised Bruce replied. "What do you want me to do?"

Mac quickly replied, "Learn it and learn it fast. We don't have the next four years to play around. The old man wants a buildable solution by Labor Day and you are going to give it to him, boy. Not me!"

Bruce looked up at the clock and saw it was after 5:00 p.m. "If you're going to catch your train, you better get out of here fast," Mac said.

Bruce didn't have to be told twice and decided to get out quickly before Mac changed his mind. "Wow, my first week is over. Maybe my project is going to get built after all. I have my work cut out for me this weekend," Bruce thought happily as he ran, loaded down with books, to the train station.

He viewed the summer of 1960 as a pivotal year in his life. Everything changed. He gave up summer nights of

Pony League Baseball. He gave up lounging around with his friends at the soda shop and the activity he loved most —summer at the Jersey Shore. His project took on a life of its own and redefined Bruce's life along the way.

Suddenly he realized and thought to himself, "My life has changed. Instead of spending the summer with my friends and family at the Shore, I'm locked up five days a week with a slave-driving Scotsman in the heat of New York City from 9:00 a.m. to 5:00 p.m. and that's not the worst of it. My family moved twenty miles away to Westfield, New Jersey. I might as well be living in China!"

Still feeling isolated and disconnected from everything that was comfortable and familiar Bruce continued with his thoughts. "Since I don't drive I can't visit my friends. At least I can get to the Jersey Central train station which takes me partway into the City. Then, instead of going into Grand Central, now I catch the ferry boat from Hoboken to lower Manhattan every day where it docks about four blocks from where I work. The good news is I can get coffee and doughnuts on the ferry ride. That's something I look forward to every morning. I know it's not the Jersey Shore but at least I have water and boats!"

Summer progressed and he and Mac found a rhythm that worked and their relationship seemed to improve. "I feel as if Mac finally accepts me," he thought one day. "I hope he realizes I'm not a freeloader. I'm willing to work hard. I come from a working class family and we aren't part of the country club scene. I don't expect anything I haven't earned. I heard through the grapevine that Mac might even like me a little bit. I will take what I can get from him."

Bruce continued to work hard and each day his drawing ability improved. Over and over again he revised his original drawings and after at least ten revisions the building design evolved from "pie in the sky" to a sound and buildable engineering solution, thanks to Mac's guidance. Every time Bruce turned in a completed set of drawings Mac scrutinized and challenged the design. "This isn't complete. More details and specifications are needed," was Mac's standard response.

Bruce, left to his own ingenuity and resources, discovered what was missing from the drawing details. "I know three sources to check," reasoned Bruce. "I can check Mac Junior's old textbooks, the complete set of Sweets Catalogs Mac got for me to use or I can go to the good, old New York Public Library."

Secretly both he and Mac looked forward to the unexpected breaks that the trip to the Library gave them. On rare occasions a special event provided a pleasant interruption to their working rhythm. Today was one of those special days. "I'm going with Mr. Kauffeld to one of his lunch appointments," he told Mac.

SHARING THE ASTRONARIUM STORY

Just like a few other times Bruce and Mr. Kauffeld met in the lobby and joined George, the chauffeur, who drove them to their destination in the limousine. "Today we're going to meet some of my friends and associates at the University Club, Bruce. I want you to give them an overview of your Astronarium and Science Center project and tell them why you feel it's so important," explained Mr. Kauffeld.

He was excited and always enjoyed the opportunity to tell his story to these important and impressive people. Today wasn't the first time. Earlier in the summer he shared his story with some of Mr. Kauffeld's friends and associates at the New York Yacht Club and at the New York Athletic Club. Each time he told his story he gained added support from the audience and he gained self-confidence as a speaker as well.

"I have never imagined myself as a speaker before. These people are actually interested in what I have to say and offer," he thought to himself. "They always seem to have positive and encouraging comments to say about me and my story."

He looked forward to the outings and welcomed the invaluable experience they offered him. He learned about the City's culture and had opportunities to interact in a variety of business and social settings. Naturally he learned new details about himself too.

One of the earlier luncheon meetings at the University Club came to mind as he thought about his experiences. "I will never forget that lunch. Everyone ordered oysters on the half shell. So, I decided to order them too. When the waiter set them down in front of me I couldn't believe it. I had no idea what I was doing and had never seen anything like them before. I didn't know what to do with them. I can't even look at them now. I was really green, literally. I did what everyone else did and ate them. All of a sudden I excused myself because I felt sick and hurried to the men's room. Never again!"

Bruce was a keen observer and always watched how people behaved and interacted as if he had been an anthropologist studying new cultures or tribes. "I believe that someday these experiences will help me with my project," he thought to himself insightfully.

He became comfortable joining Mr. Kauffeld during these luncheon meetings. "Mr. Kauffeld always seems pleased with the outcome of the meetings and he always asks me for a project update on the way back to the office," Bruce reflected. "This way I can let him know that we are on schedule and that I'm getting along very well with Mac."

A comfortable routine and rhythm was created and as the summer ended and Labor Day passed Mac sat with Bruce and said, "Let's go over all of the documents that you have prepared."

Bruce prepared himself. He thought, "This is going to be like all of the other reviews and Mac will tell me to do it again."

But it turned out differently that day. Mac surprised him and announced, "Well, you are done, Mr. Tully! You have done a man's job, sir. It may not look pretty, but this building can be built beam by beam! We will leave the pretty stuff to the architects. Congratulations, Bruce. I will set up an appointment for your presentation with Mr. Kauffeld and the Executive Board."

Bruce could hardly believe what he heard and asked, "Will you come too, Mac?"

"Oh no, that's front office stuff. That's not my cup of tea," Mac told Bruce. "Don't worry. There isn't anything here you can't answer. You will do just fine. Now get on with you or you will miss your boat!"

As he left Mac and walked quickly to the ferry Bruce remembered their conversation. "He didn't call me 'boy' one time. He called me 'Mr. Tully' and said I did a man's job! Wow! Mac's confidence and approval mean a lot to me."

The summer of 1960 was definitely a rite of passage for Bruce. He began the summer as a sixteen-year-old boy who ventured into New York City all alone with nothing more than a big box tied with a fuzzy cord, some rolled-up drawings and determination. As the summer was ending Bruce had grown into a young man full of professional confidence. He was ready to embrace the unknown and thought to himself, "Wait until Mom and Dad hear what Mac said. I'm done! Tonight will be my treat at Spirito's."

ENTER THE ARCHITECTS

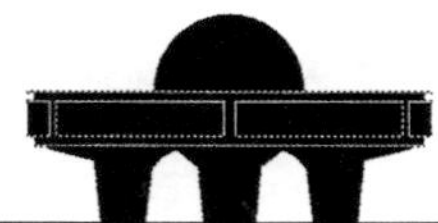

After enjoying another family celebration that evening and a great weekend when Monday rolled around it was clear to Bruce that it was time for his project to move to the next step. TJK was ready to call in the architects. Mr. Kauffeld scheduled lunch and included time for a presentation with a highly respected design firm, La Pierre and Litchfield. Their offices were in Midtown. They were located in a two-story penthouse office at the top of a beautiful art deco building. Bruce realized that they were right across the street from one of his favorite resting places that he had found earlier in the summer when he trudged around the City carrying his box and rolled-up drawings. It was a small public park behind The New York City Library! "This is a good sign," he thought.

When they arrived and entered the offices Bruce noticed the differences in the office space immediately. "This office is really comfortable and feels relaxing compared to the sparse utilitarian office where I've been working. It sure beats Mac's back room," he thought.

He continued his observations and speculation. "If you're a chief design architect for this place, you probably come from one of the Ivy League schools like Yale, Harvard, Cornell or the University of Pennsylvania," he guessed.

Soft, classical music played in the background and many kinds of refreshments were displayed beautifully on trays. All of the key people finally joined the TJK team and everyone moved into a conference room.

Bruce met Mr. Litchfield, his son Laurence and Wes Weidner. Bruce later learned that Wes Weidner was viewed as one of the current, rising architectural stars.

The Litchfields came from a long line of what Bruce called American blue-blooded aristocracy dating back to the direct descendants of the colonial family of Litchfields who founded Litchfield, Connecticut.

He watched the three men during lunch to see how they handled themselves. He always observed and stored away information that he might be able to use in the future.

As he presented his story he observed the reactions from the architects and waited for comments and feedback. He thought, "Weidner seems full of himself and he knows he's good."

Mr. Litchfield was the first to speak, "Ted, thank you for a lovely lunch today. You and Mr. Tully certainly have a very interesting story to tell. Exactly how do you think we can help you?"

Although he seemed curious Bruce felt his tone was a little condescending. "Litchfield reminds me of a typical New

Englander who can speak whole sentences through tightly clenched teeth without moving his lips. Am I the only one that sees this?" wondered Bruce.

Tuning back into the conversation he heard Mr. Kauffeld answer, "Bruce has taken his plan as far as he can without the help of a professional architectural design team. I was hoping that you could see your way clear to evaluate it and see if you can make it your own without sacrificing the basic concept."

Looking over at Wes who was nodding his head 'yes,' the senior Litchfield turned to his son and asked, "What do you think about it, Larry?"

Larry answered, "Working with Bruce will be fun. Sure, why not? When do we start?"

"Count us in, Ted," said the senior Litchfield. "How about starting tomorrow? Is that soon enough?"

Laughing, everyone stood up and shook hands on the agreement. Bruce spoke for the first time and asked, "Where will I work?"

Larry answered, "Why, here, of course!"

He was excited and happy. He tried to hold it down though. After all, he was in a meeting with some very high-powered professionals and wanted to be viewed as a professional too. "At last I'm free from Mac's window-less prison cell," he thought.

Later he learned he would work on the upper level of the penthouse suite right next to two huge glass doors that opened onto a balcony overlooking the Empire State

Building just a few blocks south. "A room with a view. This is where the beautiful people work and I can even see the Statue of Liberty," he thought to himself. "There's no comparison to where I've been working. It doesn't get any better than this!"

On the ride back to TJK Mr. Kauffeld said, "MacCabe told me that you stood up under all of his pressure throughout the summer. He thinks you have great potential and so do I. We want you to remain at TJK until we present the project in Washington next year. Litchfield thinks it will take until January to complete all of the necessary work. I agree with him. So, I'm giving you a raise to eighty-five dollars a week and I'm prepared to help you go to school here in New York. This will help you continue with your important work, Bruce. I want to meet with your parents and discuss my proposal with them. What do you think?"

Bruce was surprised at this turn of events and couldn't believe what he heard. "Really, Mr. Kauffeld, you want me to stay on at TJK and work with the architects at the same time? I'm in. I'm ready," responded Bruce.

Bruce and Mr. Kauffeld were in agreement. They were ready to take the Astronarium and Science Center project forward immediately. "Let's do it," said Mr. Kauffeld.

When they returned to the office Mr. Kauffeld asked his secretary to contact Bruce's parents and invite them to lunch. Later in the week they all met at the University Club where he presented his idea and proposal to Bruce's parents. It was quickly agreed that Bruce could continue his work on his

Astronarium project during the Fall and attend school in New York City. His life was going through some major changes. Mr. Kauffeld told his parents that he contacted the Headmaster of the prestigious Rhodes Preparatory School in Manhattan and discussed Bruce's situation with him.

ENTER THE ARCHITECTS 159

BEDLAM!

Given Bruce's unique mission and situation the Headmaster agreed to the plan and was fully supportive. Rhodes was known as the school of choice for working professional students in New York City. Many of its students were young performers who were involved in various forms of entertainment including theater and television. The school offered a program that included intensive classroom study in the morning which allowed students to be dismissed at noon. Students were free to pursue their professional careers in the afternoons and evenings.

It sounded perfect; however, it turned out to be somewhat of a culture shock for Bruce. He was used to going to a public high school in New Jersey. "I thought that wandering the streets of the City looking for project sponsors was culture shock. It was nothing compared to Rhodes. Man, every day I'm faced with flakes, fruits and nuts. All of them must be here. Everyone is eccentric. There's a clique of gay chorus boys who spend most of their time hurling sexual insults at one another. A group of orthodox Jewish kids sit around in class always studying the Talmud and doing homework. Some here think they're special but I call them precocious. They're geniuses—thirteen- and fourteen-year-olds who already have been accepted to Harvard and MIT. They will be full PhDs by the time they are nineteen. Unbelievable!

Then there are the entertainers—the biggest drama kings and queens who look for attention from everyone including the teachers and staff.

Oh, yeah, standing out are the New York elite ultra-rich kids who think they rule everyone!

Where do I fit in?" he asked himself.

"I don't fit in," he realized. "The truth is that I don't want to fit into this place!"

He thought about Rhodes and his observations. "I stand out like a sore thumb. They think I'm from another planet. No athletes are here. The only sports at this place are chess and the debate team. I don't have anything in common with anyone," he realized.

Bruce felt isolated and alone at Rhodes. "I miss my old friends and teammates. Rhodes isn't anything special and I don't like it," he thought. "I can stand it if this is the price I have to pay to keep my mission for the Astronarium and Science Center alive."

He began to think of Rhodes as nothing more than biding his time. The only time he really enjoyed was after school when he worked. This made it all worthwhile.

One day, to his delight, he met a beautiful, petite, blonde actress whose name was Jill Haworth. She had just finished a part in the epic film *Exodus*. Jill had played the character of Karen opposite Sal Mineo. She was different, shy, a little aloof, nice and a real actress. She wasn't like the other kids. She was pretty down-to-earth as far as Bruce was concerned. Soon he and Jill found they both hated Rhodes and quickly became friends.

Every day they waited for the twenty-minute break. Then they raced up Fifth Avenue to the Plaza Hotel at the edge of Central Park. Jill smoked a forbidden cigarette and they enjoyed some refreshments. Some days they cut their remaining morning classes and went to the newly opened Guggenheim Museum or the famous Metropolitan Museum of Art. There they wandered around and looked at the beautiful collections of art. Jill softly and quietly shared her knowledge of the art world with Bruce while he listened attentively to every word.

A PROFESSIONAL PASSION IS DISCOVERED

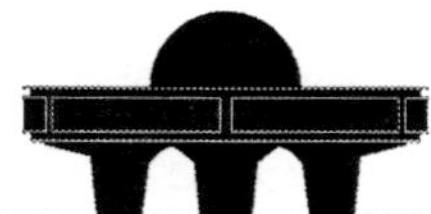

Bruce was impatient during morning classes. He counted the minutes until it was time to escape to his real love, the offices of LP&L. He took the subway or sometimes rode the red double-decked bus that traveled up and down Fifth Avenue. He enjoyed the ride and could see all of the beautiful high-rises.

He didn't miss the sterile and utilitarian environment of Mac's office. His new environment felt sophisticated and everyone at LP&L seemed like the perfect picture of up and coming, trendy design professionals. "What a contrast!" he thought. "I'm grateful to be here."

At LP&L Bruce was welcomed. He was treated with respect and dignity, like an aspiring young designer with lots of potential and just like any other member of the team. He loved every minute of the time he spent there. He also learned to appreciate the fine art of drinking imported espresso and eating appetizers for snacks during coffee breaks. "I feel as though I've died and gone to heaven," he sighed.

A design team was created to transform his elementary and buildable concept into an award-winning building that could hold its own against other iconic artifacts in the world like the Eiffel Tower and Frank Lloyd Wright's Guggenheim Museum.

The team was made up of lead designers, Larry Litchfield and Wes Weidner. It included a drafting team with Ted Paderewski, a young architectural engineering student and Achiem Mohammed aka Mr. Jefferson or "Jeff" Brown, a young, large black architect who was obsessed with the preaching of Malcolm X. Bruce was added as a third draftsman thanks to his quick study and education with Mac.

The team members referred to Wes as "W" who said, "I'm not going to be happy with any results unless we get this published in one of the professional journals. Unless we make *The Record* or *Progressive Architecture* you're nobody. I don't care how good you think your product is," he said bringing the team back to reality.

A schedule was created with dates to complete the conceptual design by the end of September. This included a definitive design and a complete outline of specifications that would be used to develop a letter of architectural and engineering opinions of cost. It was scheduled to be completed by the end of November. Everyone was excited to begin the next phase of the project.

Bruce consulted on the design and drafted the refined drawings. He was the liaison between the engineering and architectural design efforts as well as the material and equipment suppliers. He thought, "This is perfect! Mac prepared me well for this responsibility. I feel as if I know the process."

His design was new and innovative. It had never been built before. Within the Astronarium he included innovative concepts for furniture and tools to view space and the stars. He enjoyed working with world-famous firms to complete his design concepts. Haywood Wakefeld finished designing the "Astrochair" and Karl Zeiss designed the Astronarium projector.

Each day brought new growth opportunities. Bruce loved seeing his concept take form. Because of this he was able to cope with school in the mornings. Not only did he feel like a valued team member. He found himself included in social events. "Wow, I get to see Cornell play against other top Ivy League teams," thought Bruce. "I had no idea this was going to happen. I think I know what I want to do when I graduate from high school now. I'm going to college and study architecture." These experiences helped Bruce shape his life in ways he had never imagined.

The team diligently worked through the Fall and by December they were done.

Bruce took a deep breath and said to himself, "It's been one year since I sat at my kitchen table and began this project. Now look at what we have accomplished—a presentation with a buildable design. I'm so grateful and excited. Look how far it's come. Instead of a cardboard box to carry my wooden model in we've created a beautiful, cushioned wooden box to carry a very detailed professional acrylic scale model wherever we go."

WE ARE READY!

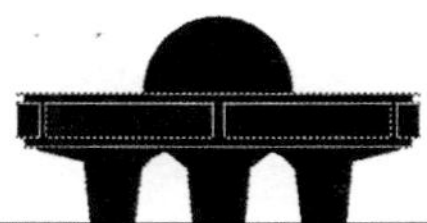

While the team worked to complete the project, Mr. Kauffeld continued to create interest with various groups. It was a week before Christmas and he called the team together for a strategic planning meeting. "Let's talk about who will be part of the first traveling team and how we will present the project to people," he began. "I have arranged for us to present our project to key officials at the Department of Commerce. Remember, they are the ones in charge of the U.S. Government's World's Fair planning and allocations in case New York City is approved as the location for the World's Fair."

After quite a bit of discussion Mr. Kauffeld quickly summarized who was on the team. "We all agree that the primary team includes Bruce, Larry, Jim and me. Now we also need someone who can continue meeting with key government and industry people, someone who is charismatic, professional and very comfortable communicating with influential people, someone to give our project visibility and gain support. They have to have the same 'can do' attitude that we have. We may have times when they will have to stand in for me when I'm not available."

This triggered a lot more discussion and thoughts about who was right for the open position—someone who was dedicated to the project's success as much as they were. A lot of names were thrown out, discussed and dismissed. They seemed to be getting nowhere.

Bruce listened carefully and considered the qualities the person needed. All of a sudden he realized who was right for the job. "Mr. Kauffeld, I know who the right person for this job is," he blurted out. "It's my Dad and he can do everything you said."

"Really?" asked Mr. Kauffeld, "Are you sure? Bruce, if you feel strongly about him, see if you can get him in to meet with me before the holidays. Our first meeting is scheduled for the ninth of January in D.C. and we need to identify our last team member before then."

"Yes, sir, I will have an answer for you tomorrow," replied Bruce.

The more Bruce thought about his Dad filling the role, the more he knew it was right. "My Dad is perfect. He looks like a movie star and he attended the American Academy of Dramatic Arts. He's been in Broadway plays, he's played major league baseball for the Philadelphia Athletics and he has been successful as a Regional Sales Manager for one of the largest pharmaceutical companies in the country. He's no stranger to talking to important people or to large groups."

"I know this is right," he thought. "It might even help my Dad out since we had to move this summer after he was passed over for a promotion. Rather than work for someone he didn't respect his Dad wanted to have time to create and produce a new private detective adventure series for television. The plan would be to film it in the capital city of Brazil because of its stunning architecture and beautiful scenery. Dad had reconnected with some of his old Hollywood connections. He had gotten permission from the Brazilian Consulate General here in New York City and all of the connections seem to be moving forward. I know my family is under some financial strain right now, so, this opportunity is perfect for him," reasoned Bruce.

He arrived home from work and while everyone was sitting around the dinner table that evening Bruce told his parents about the opportunity. At first his Dad was reluctant and responded coolly. "I'm no charity case!"

Bruce persisted, "Dad, this is no charity case. We need you, your skills and your experience to be part of the team. We need one more person. Why not you? You have a lot to add to this project."

The more they discussed it Bruce sensed some of his Dad's resistance leaving. "Just meet with Mr. Kauffeld, Dad. It's only one meeting. If you don't like what he has to say, then you can always say 'no.'"

Bruce's Mom jumped in and offered her opinion. "Tony, I think you should meet with him. You have nothing to lose."

Finally he agreed to the meeting. Bruce was relieved and arranged it with Mr. Kauffeld. They met just before Christmas. Time was of the essence. The meeting went well. It was settled. His Dad became part of the team, a special consultant. He reported to Mr. Kauffeld and he could continue developing his television project.

Bruce was happy and pleased at the way all the details were shaping up. "This is going to be the best Christmas and New Year ever," he thought. "I still can't believe how far we have come since last year at this time. It feels like a miracle to me. Now we can really enjoy the holidays!"

BACK TO WORK!

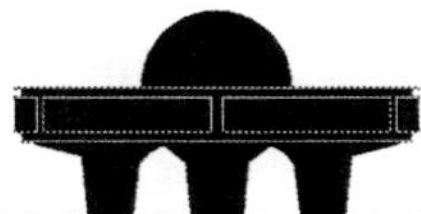

The holidays passed quickly and it was time to return to work. The offices of TJK bustled with excitement about the upcoming trip to meet with the Department of Commerce in Washington, D.C. Bruce thought that Mr. Kauffeld was a miracle worker. He arranged for them to meet with the highest members of the department including the incoming and outgoing Secretaries of Commerce and their key staff members.

As the team discussed the upcoming trip Mr. Kauffeld turned to his secretary and asked, "Paula, please make travel arrangements for our trip. I want the entire team to travel in the parlor car with me on the Washingtonian Express from Penn Station to D.C. Then make reservations to stay at the Hay Adams Hotel. It's across the street from the White House."

"Wow, the parlor car and the Hay Adams Hotel! It's really well known and very prestigious. We're traveling in style," thought an excited Bruce.

"Bruce, I want you to go up to Brooks Brothers this afternoon. George will take you. It's in Midtown right behind Grand Central Station. When you get there ask for Mel. He's my personal tailor, and he will know what to do for you," explained Mr. Kauffeld.

"Yes, sir," responded an excited Bruce.

Turning back to his secretary he said, "Call George and see to it that he takes Bruce Uptown."

Without hesitation she picked up the phone and made arrangements with George. "Bruce, George will be waiting for you out in front of the building in thirty minutes."

"Thank you. I will be there," he responded.

When Bruce arrived out in front of the building thirty minutes later he immediately saw George and the limo waiting. During the ride Uptown a light snowfall flickered down and Bruce looked out the windows and appreciated the holiday decorations remaining in the stores. "This feels like New York City at its best," he thought.

Before he knew it they were at Brooks Brothers. He stepped inside the store looking around for someone to ask about Mel. He approached the first salesperson he met and explained, "I'm supposed to see Mel. Mr. Kauffeld sent me."

He was shown to a sitting area where he waited. Before long he saw a trim and slightly balding man walking toward him. As the man approached he offered his hand to Bruce. As they shook hands he said, "Hello, I'm Mel. How can I help you?"

"Mr. Kauffeld sent me and said I should ask for you. My name is Bruce."

"Of course. Mr. Kauffeld called and told me about your upcoming trip and what you will need. Come with me and we will get you fitted," replied Mel.

Bruce was amazed. Things happened so fast. An executive fitting at Brooks Brothers was quite an experience. This was a first and he knew he was in good hands. As they went into the fitting area he saw a tailor waiting with his assistant. "I wonder what I do now. I've never been fitted for a suit before. They do things first-class here. Not only do they have private fittings. They offer their customers coffee and refreshments," he thought.

Bruce discovered that Mr. Kauffeld had told Mel exactly what he wanted him to wear for this very important meeting. He was fitted with a British dark gray herringbone suit, a white, high-stitched count Pima cotton button-down collared shirt and black wing-tipped shoes. Everything was waiting and ready for him to try on. In addition Mel brought in a selection of very expensive silk ties for Bruce to choose from. "This is something I can do," he thought.

He tried on the suit and shirt and experimented with the ties. Finally he decided on a rich dark navy tie with silver accents. "This will go with my suit perfectly," he thought to himself.

"Now for the finishing touch," said Mel. "Here's a beautiful, black Chesterfield overcoat and felt hat."

"I feel like a million bucks," thought Bruce as the tailor pinned and tucked the adjustments to his new clothes.

"We will have these delivered to your office tomorrow," offered Mel.

"That's great," responded a surprised Bruce. "What do I owe you for all of this?"

"Nothing, Bruce. Mr. Kauffeld has taken care of everything and put it on his tab—something about a Christmas present, I think he said," replied Mel.

Bruce was very surprised and exclaimed, "Well, then, I guess that's even better!"

As he left Brooks Brothers Bruce noticed the time. "That seemed to take a long time, but I've only been here thirty minutes. That was an amazing experience," he thought. "Now let me find George. Ah, there he is, right out in front. I'm not surprised."

"George, may I ask you for a small favor? Would you drop me off at Rockefeller Center? I have something that I need to do," explained Bruce.

"Sure, Bruce, no problem," answered George.

A SHORT BREAK

George dropped him off on Fifth Avenue and he walked down the mall which led to the Christmas tree and skating rink below. He had arranged to meet his friend, Jill, from Rhodes Academy for a cup of hot chocolate and a little ice skating. Anticipating seeing Jill again, Bruce walked quickly and thought, "I haven't seen her for almost a month because of the Christmas break at school. I'm looking forward to seeing her again."

As he neared the ice rink he saw her waiting and felt happy. They greeted each other with a big hug and she gave him a small kiss on his cheek which seemed to be a British custom. Jill was British. They moved to the Rockefeller Café and sat down still laughing and talking non-stop. They ordered hot chocolate and began to catch up with each other and share what was going on in their lives.

After finishing their hot chocolate they decided to ice-skate. Enjoying the break and each others' company they skated hand in hand. Sometimes they fell down and because they felt so carefree they laughed and giggled just like little kids. The time together seemed magical to both of them.

Although neither one of them realized it, this would be the last time they saw one another. Jill was destined to go to Hollywood soon where she would become a successful star and Bruce wouldn't be returning to Rhodes Academy. Because of an upcoming, extraordinary and unexpected busy schedule he was going to take a leave of absence from Rhodes. For the moment, however, time stood still while they cherished one another's company on a dark and snowy December afternoon. Time passed too quickly and soon it was time to say "good-bye."

TRAVELING IN STYLE

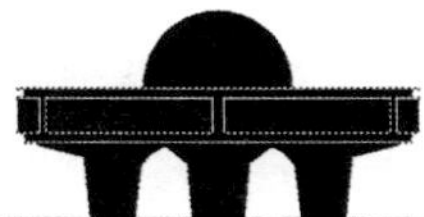

Bruce returned to the office and wasted no time finding Mr. Kauffeld. "Thank you so much for your generosity and the experience at Brooks Brothers," he said.

"You're welcome, Bruce," responded a smiling and pleased Mr. Kauffeld.

As the days passed the weather remained damp and cold. January arrived and it was time to head for Washington, D.C. The team stood on the platform at Penn Station waiting to take the Washingtonian Express. Steam bellowed out of the engine and seemed to cover the platform in an eerie mist. Porters hustled up and down the platform yelling commands and directions to one another. Conductors were stationed at the entrance of each car so they could direct passengers to their seats. As far as Bruce was concerned this was luxury at its best. A seat in the parlor car was considered beyond luxurious.

The group boarded the train and entered the parlor car. Bruce looked around, taking in everything. "This is better than first class," he thought to himself.

Everywhere he looked he saw luxury. The floors were covered with plush Oriental rugs. Rich draperies hung on the walls. He noticed large, overstuffed leather swivel chairs and strategically located tables for reading or playing cards. At one end of the car a large, full-service bar was ready and at the other end of the car was the entrance into a private dining car for parlor guests only.

"All aboard," they heard the conductor shout.

"We're on our way," thought Bruce as the train pulled out of the station for the two-and-a-half-hour trip to Washington, D.C.

As they traveled the air in the parlor car filled with a rich aroma of expensive imported cigars. Waiters in white coats soon came around taking drink orders and Bruce noticed that many travelers ordered the best single malt scotch and rye whiskey.

Before long card games started and Bruce thought, "This is a gentleman's country club on rails. The parlor car is even better than riding in the limo!"

Later the team retired to the dining car to enjoy a fine dinner of oysters on the half shell, vichyssoise, and chateaubriand followed by dessert—Southern bread pudding smothered in rum sauce. "Leave it to Mr. Kauffeld," he thought. "He sure knows how to do things first class!"

Time seemed to pass quickly and before he knew it the train pulled into Washington's National Train Station. The team loaded themselves into cabs and headed directly to the Hay Adams Hotel. The hotel was famous and known as the watering hole of the Washington power elite. Bruce noticed the impressive White House across the street from the hotel as they pulled up.

They were greeted by the front desk manager as they entered the hotel lobby. "Good evening, Mr. Kauffeld. We have your regular suite ready for you. Your guests have rooms located on the same floor."

It was obvious Mr. Kauffeld traveled and stayed here frequently. Everyone said their "good-byes" after checking in. They went up to their rooms to unpack and agreed to meet in the lobby bar for a night-cap in thirty minutes.

Bruce and his Dad shared a room overlooking the White House and they saw the lights in the windows. Looking out his hotel room window Bruce wondered, "What is the President doing right now?"

They unpacked their things and Bruce and his Dad headed down to the lobby bar. He noticed how beautiful and well appointed it was. At one end of the room was a pianist who played quiet music. The other team members were gathering around a few tables so they joined them.

The team discussed their strategy for the meeting scheduled for the following morning. They talked about who they were meeting and what role each member of the team would play. They felt prepared and decided to call it a night. It had been a long day and tomorrow's meeting was extremely important.

They said their "goodnights" and headed back to their rooms. Once Bruce and his Dad entered their room his Dad said, "Okay, Bruce, let's get some sleep. Tomorrow is an important day."

"Okay, Dad," Bruce replied.

He was so excited, though, that he couldn't go to sleep right away. All he did was toss and turn. He felt his thoughts were spinning around and around inside of his head. He was so restless that sleep continued to elude him. He thought about the White House, only one hundred yards away, and the presentation that the team would give the next morning. The next thing he heard was his Dad saying, "Bruce, get some sleep. It's game day!"

"Okay, Dad," and he finally nodded off to sleep.

DEPARTMENT OF COMMERCE COMMITTEE PRESENTATION

The next thing Bruce remembered was the sound of the telephone ringing. He looked around, located the phone and answered while he looked at the clock. It was 6:30 a.m. "This is your wake-up call," said the voice on the other end.

Bruce and his Dad got up and prepared for the day. They went down to the lobby to meet the others for breakfast and before they knew it they were all on their way to the Department of Commerce for their nine o'clock meeting. "At last," Bruce thought, "we will unveil the Astronarium and Science Center!"

When they arrived they were met by several government officials. Immediately they were escorted into a large conference room. One of the high-ranking officials spoke first. "Ted, I understand you have something very interesting to share with us today. Why don't you tell us all about it?"

"Of course," he replied standing up in a way that drew everyone's attention, ensuring that his audience was captivated.

He began at the beginning and told the story from when Bruce first contacted him after meeting with Dr. Spaght of Shell Oil US. He explained everything that had transpired since then up to the presentation they would see today. After he was sure that everyone was up to speed he turned to Bruce and said, "Why don't you give them the details on just how and why you were motivated to do what you did beginning in 1959?"

"Yes, sir," Bruce responded. Then he presented a detailed accounting of events that included his motivation and all of the activities that had taken place up until the time he met Mr. Kauffeld.

Next it was Larry's turn. He told the group how his design team took Bruce's original work and evolved the design into an innovative and beautiful building that they would soon see. Larry then turned the meeting back to Bruce so that he could walk everyone through the details of the entire project.

Bruce told the story from the point of view of an arriving visitor to the Astronarium and Science Center. He walked them through the whole place explaining many details so they could see them through a visitor's eyes.

Then it was Jim's turn at bat. He reviewed building details, how the building would be built, and he included the engineers' opinions of costs.

During the entire time Bruce's Dad observed each person's reaction to what was presented. He carefully listened to their comments. Then it came time for Mr. Kauffeld to close the discussion.

The entire presentation took about three hours and now it was the officials' turn. First, they complimented Bruce for an extraordinary effort and called him a true young American patriot. Then one of the officials said, "This was more than we expected, Ted. You've thought of every detail. We need something like this. As you know, the whole city is getting ready for a Presidential administration change. Once JFK takes office a committee will be formed to study and select a solution for the United States' participation in the upcoming World's Fair."

Next Nathan Ostrof spoke. "Given the educational nature of the project it will find support. If some of the leading scientific minds like Dr. Edward Teller and Wernher von Braun would give it their support, that would carry a great deal of weight with the new committee."

Bruce's Dad interrupted at this point and asked, "Can you go into a little more detail?"

Mr. Ostrof agreed and continued to offer additional and valuable advice to the team. The meeting adjourned promptly at noon and in true Kauffeld style a reservation was booked at the Old Ebbit Grill, one of the oldest restaurants in Washington, D.C., just a stone's throw from the hotel where they were staying.

The team left the meeting and reconvened at the Grill where they went over the presentation and the feedback they received. "All in all I think the meeting was a great success," said Mr. Kauffeld to the team. "We couldn't have asked for a better response."

He turned to the waiter and said, "My good man, bring champagne for everyone!"

As their glasses were filled and raised for a toast, Mr. Kauffeld declared, "To Bruce and the Astronarium and Science Center. Hear! Hear!"

Everyone responded enthusiastically. "It's my turn," Bruce thought as he turned to Mr. Kauffeld. "Thank you for all that you have done!"

The team responded once again, "Hear! Hear!"

After lunch was finished the team checked out of the hotel and headed to the train station. "More parlor car," enthused Bruce. "This train car is too cool!"

Even though the train trip home was uneventful, Bruce and the team's spirits remained high.

APPEARING ON THE *TODAY SHOW*

It was back to business as usual the next day. Bruce was back at work and found himself thinking about the presentation when his phone buzzed. It was Mr. Kauffeld's secretary, Paula. "Bruce, I have a man on the phone who wants to talk to you. He says he's from the *Today Show*. Shall I put him through?"

Sounding surprised Bruce said, "Yes, of course, put him through!"

He realized some of the New York papers had run stories about him and his recent trip to Washington. He was in the news! Apparently one of the stories caught Dave Garroway's attention which prompted the call from the *Today Show*. "Am I speaking to Bruce Tully?" asked the voice on the other end of the line.

"Yes, you are," responded Bruce.

"We have an opening next Monday morning and would like for you to be on the *Today Show*. Mr. Garroway would like to do a short spot on you and your project. Are you available?" asked the voice.

Bruce thought to himself, "Holy smokes! We were just in Washington two days ago and now the *Today Show* is calling me! Word sure travels fast."

"Of course, I would be delighted to appear with Mr. Garroway. Does he want me to bring anything special?" asked Bruce.

"We saw a wonderful rendering of the building in the paper. Do you have anything else we can see?" inquired the voice.

"Yes, we have a very good model and full scale mock-up of the chair I designed. I call it the Astrochair," explained Bruce.

"It sounds as though those would be great to bring for the spot on the show," replied the voice. "Can you bring them with you?"

"Yes, I can," responded Bruce enthusiastically.

The call ended and Bruce thought, "Wow, I'm going to be on national TV with Dave Garroway on the *Today Show*! This is unreal!"

He immediately went searching for Mr. Kauffeld to tell him what had just happened. "That's great news, Bruce," said Mr. Kauffeld. "Be sure to mention the firm's name too!"

"Don't worry about that, Mr. Kauffeld. You know I will, several times even!"

"Once is enough, Bruce," responded Mr. Kauffeld.

Bruce was excited and couldn't wait to tell his parents about this new development. His Dad offered to help him prepare for the interview. He had a lot of experience in front of people and handled himself well. He had gone to college to become an actor and his classmates included Kirk Douglass, Humphrey Bogart, Lauren Bacall, and Burt Lancaster. His Dad's training and experience proved to be invaluable.

This was serious business as far as his Dad was concerned. He was skilled and charismatic and wanted Bruce to be as prepared as possible. Their practice was a *Today Show* simulation. His Dad instructed him on how to sit and gesture. He coached him not to look into the camera. He reminded Bruce that twenty million Americans would be listening to the show and he only had five minutes to get his points across.

His Dad explained, "Garroway will have a teleprompter with his questions scrolling down. You have to dodge and parry them to get your points across. Garroway has an agenda and might try to intimidate you. Be polite, but remember you have your message to get across."

They role-played. His Dad played Garroway and interviewed Bruce. They rehearsed his message over and over again until Bruce had it down pat. This preparation time was critical. Bruce was fortunate that his Dad was so helpful and accomplished.

COAST TO COAST

On the morning of the *Today Show* interview Bruce was due at NBC studios by 6:00 a.m. This meant he needed to be up at 3:00 a.m. It was going to be a long day. His Dad went with him and as soon as Bruce arrived at the studio he was immediately greeted by an assistant producer who took him to a room for makeup. He remembered to wear a blue shirt because he was told it would photograph better for TV. After makeup he was shown into the green room and waited for his time to go on.

After about thirty minutes the same assistant producer came into the room quickly and said, "Come on, you're up. It's time to go."

Bruce was hustled quickly out to the set which seemed very small. Dave Garroway sat on a tall stool and wore a tweed sports jacket with a blue shirt and a red bow tie. Bruce noticed all of the details. He saw his model sitting on a pedestal close to Mr. Garroway. A rendering was behind it. The Astrochair sat to the right of Garroway and an empty stool was on his left. Bruce walked over to that stool.

He sat on the stool and was wired with a microphone. His clothes and makeup were adjusted. Then he heard a loud booming voice on the set: "We're less than one minute. One minute."

Garroway looked at Bruce, leaned over close to him and said, "Do you see that camera right in front of you? Well, when that little red light next to the lens goes on, twenty million Americans will be sitting at their breakfast tables, coast to coast, looking right back at you!"

Suddenly the loud voice boomed again: "We're on countdown."

The cameraman reached his hand out with five fingers displayed and said, "Five, four, three, two, one," showing Garroway a closed fist. This was the "go" signal.

The red light flashed on and Bruce stared with his eyes wide back at the camera. He felt like a deer must feel when caught in the headlights of a car. For a moment he froze. His mind went blank and he couldn't remember his own name. A paper scroll began to roll over the top of the camera where all of Garroway's questions were written down. It was just as his Dad had said it would be.

Although he was nervous Bruce snapped back into the present and quickly remembered his Dad's coaching and the practice from the night before. "You will have less than five minutes to tell your story, not answer his silly questions! You have to take control of the interview. No matter what questions he asks, you find a way to get your own points across. For example, 'I'm glad you asked that question, Mr. Garroway,' and then tell them what you want them to know about your project. Remember your main talking points: Khrushchev; you designed it on your own at school; why you designed it; New York City walk-about; Theodore J. Kauffeld; La Pierre and Litchfield; Haywood Wakefield and the Astrochair; and the World's Fair. You have to hit all eight points in five minutes, Bruce. Don't let Garroway distract you from your mission."

Instantly Bruce became mission-focused and managed to hit all of the eight points despite the questions that Garroway asked and that were scrolling down the teleprompter. He felt as though he nailed it.

He looked over to the side and saw his Dad give him a "thumbs up" with a big smile on his face. Bruce felt great. That's all he needed to see. He knew right then the *Today Show* interview was a success.

A STANDING OVATION

After the show Bruce headed in to TJK. He made his way through the drafting room and headed back to what he considered the MacCabe dungeon. There were hundreds of small cubicles along the way. They were the homes for all of the employees. Bruce thought his workplace resembled a small United Nations. It included diverse groups of people representing many ethnicities, cultures and ages. It seemed like a melting pot. Usually each group kept to themselves and rarely noticed him.

Today was different as he walked to his office area. "They are all standing up and smiling. They seem so happy," he thought as he heard thundering applause and loud cheers.

Everyone in the office was cheering for him! He felt like a young American champion in that moment. All of these people came together united with one purpose and focus: to honor Bruce.

The more he listened to the applause and saw the genuine appreciation and pride on the people's faces he became a little emotional and didn't think he could speak. He smiled, nodded his head and said, "Thank you," as he continued to walk to his desk. He was amazed at the warm reception from the people he saw every day.

"I wonder if Jill saw me on TV. I guess I know how she feels when she's in front of a camera now. I feel as if I have just won an Olympic Gold Medal. I'm committed to see this project through more than ever," he vowed.

A NEW PRESIDENT BRINGS HOPE

This was an exciting time filled with many surprises, not only for Bruce but for the entire country. The first Roman Catholic President was about to take office. He was young and charismatic. The energy of hope infused everyone everywhere.

It was Friday night, January 20, 1961, and the whole Tully family sat glued to the TV. They witnessed the inauguration of John F. Kennedy on the steps of the nation's Capitol Building. "I can't believe what I'm seeing," thought Bruce. "A young Irish and Roman Catholic President! Things are about to change."

As he watched the ceremony, he thought about his own heritage. On his mother's side of the family his roots could be traced back to Ireland through the Dunleavy Clan—all first-generation Americans who arrived at the turn of the century. JFK's words began to penetrate through his thoughts at that moment and he heard, "Do not ask what your country can do for you. Ask what you can do for your country!"

As he heard the President's words Bruce felt as though he had been struck by lightning. He began to repeat JFK's words over and over to himself.

Then he turned to his Mom and asked, "Did you hear that? Did you hear what he just said? That's what I did, Mom. That's exactly what I did!"

Not wanting to miss a word of what the new President was saying, his Mom whispered, "Yes, yes. Shush. Be quiet." Then she turned back to watch the ceremony on TV.

Bruce heard all he needed to hear and thought, "This new President and I are on the same page. From now on I'm a Kennedy guy, no matter what."

He had no idea that in a matter of a few weeks he would understand very clearly just how in synch they were. With approval from school and his parents Bruce took a semester's leave of absence from Rhodes and remained focused on his project. It was February and winter seemed as though it would never end. He was tired of the wet and cold. The dreariness seemed to hang on. He worked in MacCabe's dungeon, as he fondly referred to his workspace.

At work and a few days after the President's speech, Bruce was summoned to the phone. It was a staff person from the Secretary of Commerce's office in Washington, D.C., calling. "Man, I wonder what they want?" he asked himself.

The answer came quickly. "Mr. Tully, we want you to join us two days from now, if you're available, to brief our staff on your project. We're meeting at the Executive Office Building in Washington at 10:00 a.m.," explained the caller.

Bruce responded enthusiastically: "Yes!"

He gathered all of the information he needed for Mr. Kauffeld, for his Mom and Dad, said his "good-byes" and went to find Mr. Kauffeld. Bruce knew his Dad was on a recruiting trip on the West Coast looking for support for the project. As he organized his thoughts he ran down the hall to the front office and found Mr. Kauffeld's secretary. "Sorry to interrupt but I need to speak with Mr. Kauffeld now," he told her.

At first she seemed perturbed and didn't want to bother Mr. Kauffeld but Bruce persisted. "It's really important that I talk to him right now."

"All right," she said reluctantly, giving in. "I'll buzz you right in."

As Bruce walked into his office, Mr. Kauffeld said, "Good morning, Bruce. I only have a minute. What's so important?"

He gave him a rundown on the call with the Commerce Secretary's staff member. Mr. Kauffeld listened and said, "Okay, Bruce, I'll check into it."

Knowing it was in good hands Bruce left and went back to work. He told his Mom about the call that night and they both were very excited about the new opportunity. He couldn't wait to get in to work the next morning and see what Mr. Kauffeld had found out.

LUNCH AT THE WHITE HOUSE

Bruce thought about meeting with the Secretary of Commerce's staff as he rode in to work. "I can't wait to hear what Mr. Kauffeld found out. This is exciting," he thought.

When he arrived and got settled in the office he was called into Mr. Kauffeld's office. Mr. Kauffeld explained, "I have made arrangements for us to fly to Washington, D.C., Bruce. This includes you and your mother. I think it's important that she joins us. We leave tomorrow morning on an early flight so I will meet you both at the Newark Airport. We're booked on Eastern Airlines Lockheed Electra Turbo jet to National Airport in D.C. and will arrive around 9:30 a.m. We can take a cab to the meeting and be there just in time for it to start at 10:00 a.m."

The flight went just as Mr. Kauffeld planned. Then events took a different turn. They were picked up at the airport and delivered to the back entrance of the White House where they were dropped off at the guard gate to check in. There they were interrogated and marched from the gate to the Executive Office Building on the White House grounds.

They were a little surprised at this turn of events and Bruce felt his heartbeat increase. He thought, "Hey, I'm at the back of the White House. No one told me anything about this. What's up?"

Next they were met by a Marine Corps guard who issued them passes into the building. "Your escort will be here in just a moment," they were told.

They clipped on their badges and waited for their escort. After a few minutes they saw a smartly dressed Marine approach the guard station. "This must be our escort," thought Bruce.

"Please follow me," said the escort as he turned and headed down a long, dark and uninspiring hallway. This was odd since the building looked very ornate from the outside and appeared to be from the Civil War era.

Bruce noticed they were only a few feet away from the White House and the new President. "Wow," he thought. "I bet he's in there right now!"

The Marine continued to lead the way and finally led the three of them into a sparsely furnished office with only a desk and two chairs. "Please wait here and don't leave the office. If you need to use the restrooms, press this intercom button and someone will escort you to the facility," they were told.

Having given them their instructions the Marine turned around crisply and closed the door as he left. He quickly returned with another chair and set it down. Then he left again. Mr. Kauffeld, Bruce and his Mom speculated on why they were waiting in this room without windows. They wondered what was going to happen in the meeting. The only decoration besides the table and three chairs for them was a picture of the President on the wall.

Bruce asked, "Mr. Kauffeld, what's going on? Do you know why we're here?"

"No, I don't, Bruce. I have no idea what's going on. It must be important, though, or we wouldn't be in this building," answered Mr. Kauffeld.

Bruce was antsy and tense. It felt weird to be told where to go and when. "We can't even leave the room and go out into the hall or to the bathroom without permission and a Marine escort. It feels as though we're prisoners," he thought to himself.

The three of them sat for thirty minutes and at 11:00 a.m. a familiar face opened the door and entered the room. It was Nathan Ostrof, one of the people who had seen their presentation in early January. "Sorry for such short notice," he said. "Things are coming together quickly around here and I could only get this time slot for this morning at the last minute. In a few minutes I will take you across the bridge to the White House."

Surprised they looked at one another and heard him explain, "I have arranged for you to have lunch with several of the President's key staffers and some of the new Commerce people. In addition, Congressman Victor Anfuso from New York has asked to meet you today. He has been following you and your work in the New York papers. Some of these people will make up the Presidential Advisory Committee for the U.S. participation in the upcoming World's Fair. I shared some of the details of your presentation that you left with me last month and they are very interested. They asked me if they could meet with you in person, so, here we are! The President is personally interested in this Fair because of the anti-propaganda value it may have to offset some of our negative press from the Communists."

He checked his watch and said, "It's time to go. Let's go."

The group left the small room and followed Ostrof back through the long corridor and across the covered walkway. At the end of the walkway they were met by another guard who checked all of their badges, pushed a button that opened an electric door into the White House.

"I can't believe we are in the White House," thought Bruce as he looked around at the hallways filled with hustling workers. "A year ago I was writing my *Manifesto* and planning my building. Now here I am standing in the White House with my Mom and Mr. Kauffeld."

Just then they were joined by three more staffers and Congressman Anfuso. Polite introductions were made by Mr. Ostrof and then one of the staffers said, "Let's go down for lunch, why don't we?"

Bruce and his Mom followed the men downstairs to a place where they were going to have lunch. It was called "The White House Mess." Bruce expected to see a place similar to his high school cafeteria. Much to his surprise they were greeted by a doorman in a dress uniform who opened the door for them and showed them into the dining room. "This is unbelievable. This dining room looks like a room right out of a French palace, the Palace of Versailles," thought Bruce.

In the center of the lavishly decorated room was a large round table. Hanging above the center of the table was one of the most beautiful and elegant crystal chandeliers Bruce had ever seen. The table was set for eight people and each seat was attended by a waiter and busman. "Man, this is something else," he thought.

They were greeted as they entered the dining room by the head waiter who spoke with a heavy French accent. "Please, Lady and Gentlemen, please sit down," he said as he showed them to their seats.

"He just gave each one of us a beautifully engraved menu for today. I can't believe what's happening," Bruce thought to himself. "I wonder what's next."

He took one look at the menu and panicked. "I can't read a word of this menu. It's all in French. Now what?"

Bruce learned that Jackie Kennedy was on a mission to bring European culture into the White House. This was quite a culture shift from the previous administration he was told. In fact during Eisenhower's time it was more of a Midwest meat and potatoes menu. "I have no idea what to order. I don't speak French and I don't want to make a mistake or look like a fool," he thought.

As he worried more about what to order he heard the door open and looked up to see who it was. "You've got to be kidding! It is the thirty-fifth President of the United States. Wow! He's walking this way. That's John F. Kennedy right here standing in front of me!"

Bruce was surprised and shocked. No one prepared him for this possibility. Everyone in the room, including Bruce, immediately stood up. Looking around the table he noticed that some of the other people were just as surprised as he was. He discovered that President Kennedy knew he was in the house and decided at the last minute to pop in and meet him in person. "Sit down, sit down, everybody," said the President motioning with his hand.

He walked directly over to Bruce's Mom and said, "You must be Mrs. Tully."

Nervously she answered, "Yes, Mr. President, I am."

"Well, Mrs. Tully, you have a son to be proud of," said the President.

Then he turned to Mr. Kauffeld and said, "You must be Ted Kauffeld."

"Yes, sir. Yes, sir, Mr. President, I am," Mr. Kauffeld said as he shook the President's hand.

Next he walked over to Bruce with everyone still standing and sat down in the empty chair next to him. "So, you're Bruce Tully," he said respectfully. "I had a chance to look at your work and, oh, yes, I saw you on the *Today Show*. Jackie and I were very impressed with how you handled yourself with Garroway. Tell me, what really motivated you to do this?"

"I wanted to make Nikita Khrushchev eat his own words, Mr. President. Last year he said that the American youth of our country are weak and stupid and he would bury all of us.

"I wanted to find a way to prove him wrong. I want to build a National Science Center, a place that stimulates and creates interest in the minds of our country's young people so they want to become scientists and engineers. This way we can hold off the threat of Communism and regain our place in the world, Mr. President," responded Bruce with power and conviction.

"Well, Bruce, you are a credit to our nation and I will personally see to it that your efforts will not go unrewarded," replied the President.

Then he paused and looked Bruce in the eyes. He leaned over slightly and asked, "If you could have me do anything in the world for you, Bruce, what would it be?"

This was so unexpected. Bruce gulped and thought, "The President of the United States, the most powerful man in the world, just asked me what he could do for me! I wasn't expecting this."

Everything seemed surreal. After a long pause and deep thought he answered carefully. "I would like to meet our astronauts and be present when we launch our first man into space."

The President looked both happy and surprised. He seemed relieved as he looked at everyone at the table. Then he said with great confidence, "I can do that!"

Everyone laughed along with the President. Turning to Bruce he said, "Let's grab some lunch now that we've settled that. What would you like to eat?"

Bruce feared this moment and decided to answer honestly looking a little sheepish, "Do you think I can have a cheeseburger and a chocolate milkshake with some fries, Mr. President?"

The President thought for a minute. He put his hand to his chin while he was thinking, sensing Bruce's discomfort with the French menu and said, "You know, Bruce, it's been a long time since a guy could get a burger and a shake around here. You know what? I think I will order one too."

Then the President looked at the others at the table indicating it was time for them to place their orders. Each of the men followed suit and ordered what Bruce and the President ordered. As all of the orders were taken Bruce noticed that the French waiter winced. He seemed affronted and a little miffed and said, "By all means, Mr. President, we will see what hamburgers we can fix!"

Turning to Bruce the President said, "You're probably going to get the best hamburger you've ever eaten, son. It will probably be made from filet mignon!"

Everyone laughed as they heard the President's comments. His Mom, however, had her eye on the Crab Louie and ordered what she wanted!

Bruce thought, "I've just experienced the impossible. I'm having lunch with the President of the United States and he said I was a credit to the nation. I feel as if I'm in a dream."

Before long it was time to leave the White House.

Sometime later on the flight home it all began to sink in. The weight of it all overwhelmed Bruce. "I'm just a sixteen-year-old kid. This past year has been full of sacrifice and hardship at school, rejection and being put to the test by a group of hardnosed engineers and architects. Today I have spent time with the President of the United States. He respected what I have done and listened to what I had to say. This is unbelievable. I never imagined this would happen when I took on Khrushchev's challenge. It has been one of the best days of my life. Does it ever get any better than this?"

As his thoughts drifted on the homeward flight Bruce recalled his Dad's stinging words: "Who do you think is going to listen to you? You're just a stupid kid from New Jersey!"

As he looked out the airplane's window Bruce whispered, "The President of the United States of America! That's who listened to me, Dad!"

Then his thoughts wandered back to his grandfather. "Thank you so much, Grandpa Joseph, for teaching me who I am and for preparing me for this mission. Today was for you, Grandpa, all for you!"

A GAUNTLET IS TOSSED

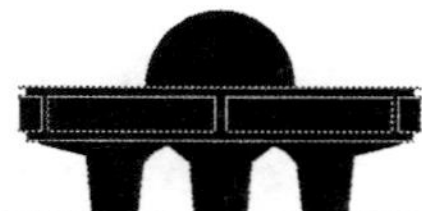

After returning from Washington it didn't take long for new events to start happening. Bruce was at work and his head was still buzzing from all of the excitement of meeting the President and presenting his project to the staff of the Secretary of Commerce.

He received an interesting call from a very influential journalist. Mr. Richard Slawsky, the science editor of the New York World Telegram and Sun, called and said, "Bruce, this is Dick Slawsky over at the Sun."

Bruce knew immediately who he was. Dick Slawsky was known as a literary giant among the scientific community of journalists, like Jules Berman and Frank McGee. He was an Andy Chaikin of his time. Bruce looked forward to reading his weekly column. He perked up. "Yes, sir, Mr. Slawsky. How can I help you?"

"Hey, call me Dick," Slawsky responded. "I would like for you to come over and talk to me. I want to ask a few questions about your project."

Bruce's name and his project were getting around town and receiving a lot of attention since he appeared on the *Today Show*. Now he was important enough to catch Slawsky's attention. "Sure. When?" asked Bruce.

"What are you doing this afternoon?" Slawsky asked.

"Today? Sure, I can make it," answered Bruce.

"Good. I will see you in my office in about thirty minutes," Slawsky said as he hung up the phone.

Bruce was aware of the value of good press so he jumped at the chance to meet with Slawsky. In a matter of minutes he left the office and arrived at the Sun's offices. Slawsky was sitting in the middle of what looked like an explosion of papers and newspapers scattered in total disarray around his tiny office. On top and in the middle of the desk sat an old-fashioned Royal upright, manual typewriter. Slawsky sat behind the desk in what seemed to be a cloud of cigarette smoke.

Taking in everything in the room quickly, Bruce noticed that Slawsky appeared to be a chain smoker. The two fingers on one hand were stained with nicotine and his other arm was missing. Slawsky was dressed in a heavy tweed sports jacket and wore wrinkled corduroy pants. He wore a sweater vest and dress shirt that was open at the collar. The whole outfit was set off by a pair of heavy, black horn-rimmed glasses with thick lenses. He was quite a sight. Bruce thought, "The way he dresses is quite a contrast to how I'm dressed in my Brooks Brothers' suit."

Slawsky was an old school beat reporter who made his way up the ladder the hard way. He had a reputation for being hard-hitting with an "in your face" attitude and approach. He didn't waste any time getting to the heart of the issue with Bruce. "All right, kid, did you do this stuff or not?"

Bruce was surprised. "Apparently the gloves are off," he thought.

"Yes, of course I did," he responded somewhat put off by Slawsky's hard-hitting style.

Slawsky pushed harder. "Yeah, right! Are you sure your old man or Kauffeld didn't put you up to all this? I see your old man is in on the gig now too."

Slawsky was a Jersey boy who had grown up tough in Jersey City, New Jersey. He was a graduate of Rutgers University, the Jersey State School. Bruce was a Jersey boy too and it didn't take long for him to get right into the groove, giving it back just as hard. After all, you know the saying: "You can take the boy out of Jersey, but you can never take Jersey out of the boy." Bruce held his own with Slawsky. The two went at each other, back and forth, for a good half-hour—two kindred spirits.

Slawsky continued to bear down on Bruce like a prosecuting attorney during cross-examination. Bruce held his own under the intense questioning and responded with facts and confidence. Finally, Slawsky let up. "Okay, okay, I believe you, kid. You are the real deal. It's an amazing thing you have done here, kid. I'm impressed, and I don't impress very easily."

Bruce took a breath and slowly sat back in his chair relaxing for the first time since he entered Slawsky's office. "Okay, but what are we doing here?"

"If I'm going to get behind you and your concept with the power of my column, I want to make sure I'm getting behind the truth, especially when it comes to some kid. I want to make sure this isn't some put-up job, cooked up by a couple of guys like your old man and Kauffeld. I want to make sure they aren't exploiting a kid while they put one over on everyone! That's what we're doing here," he explained.

Bruce nodded and said, "Okay. I understand now. Honest, my Dad had nothing to do with this. In the beginning he told me I was just a stupid kid from Jersey and nobody would even listen to me. He didn't even want me to go into the City last year. My Mom had to talk him into it. As far as Mr. Kauffeld goes, he had no idea who I was until Dr. Spaght called him last summer and told him to see me. I kid you not, man! I sold Spaght and Kauffeld on the project all by myself."

"Okay, okay. Calm down," said Slawsky. "I've decided to get behind your project and cover your story from now until the ball game is over based on our meeting today. You've convinced me. I know you've had some good coaches up until now in the areas of engineering and architecture. You're going to need a real expert in your corner when it comes to media relations and the political spin process.

If this thing goes the way I think it's going to go, the national media is going to be all over you. They will sleep in your front yard, kid, just to get to you. The story you tell is a pretty good story but if it gets out there in the wrong hands, these guys will turn on you like a pack of hyenas and rip you to shreds. You're playing in the big leagues now, kid."

Bruce became more serious as he listened to Slawsky. "Then there's the matter of Robert Moses. Your team has taken on one of the toughest, hardest, top dogs in New York City. You guys went out there and invited yourselves into Moses's party without an invitation. I'm not exactly sure how that's going to play out, but right now I'm sure he isn't happy at all about all the attention that you're getting. He likes being the whole show. Right now you're nothing but a side show to him. Rumors are he will be taking his own proposal to Washington for HIS vision of how the USA will fit into HIS Fair! Starting to get my drift, kid?"

Bruce was thoughtful as he listened and asked, "Well, who do I need to get to help me with this stuff?"

"You're looking at him, kid," Slawsky responded as he sat back taking another deep draw on his cigarette. He put it out, looked at Bruce and smiled as he immediately lit another one.

"Really, why would you do that? You've been beating me down since I entered your office," Bruce questioned.

"I like you, kid. I like your spunk. You're a street fighter deep down inside, just like me, in spite of that suit you're wearing. You're what I hoped you would be when I invited you over here. Besides I think you really have a great idea and the kids of this country really need this. Whenever I write my column I think that maybe some kid out there might actually be reading it and taking it to heart. Maybe the next U.S.-born Wernher von Braun is reading me. You see, kid, we're talking to the same audience, you and me. Besides, you're a sincere kid and I don't want to see you get hurt."

From that day forward, Richard "Dick" Slawsky was in Bruce's corner providing expert media and political advice. He coached Bruce and prepped him before every major event including writing supportive articles in his column. He was a great advocate and wanted the Astronarium and Science Center to succeed.

His first story appeared after meeting with Bruce on February 8, 1961. Dick Slawsky became one of Bruce's key mentors along with Ted Kauffeld, Albert MacCabe, and Larry Litchfield.

A PROMISE KEPT

February seemed to go by quickly and brought with it another surprise toward the end of the month. Bruce received another call. This time it was from Captain James Sparks, United States Air Force. As he listened he heard, "My name is Captain Sparks. We have just received orders that will involve our office's logistical support. It's important if you can join us at our Fifth Avenue office today."

A surprised and intrigued Bruce said, "If you give me your address I will be there by 2:00 p.m. Will that work?"

"Yes, that will work," replied Captain Sparks.

Wondering what the meeting was about, Bruce arrived at the office and was immediately greeted by Captain Sparks and the office Commander, Major Housman. Wasting no time the Major said, "Bruce, you have received a top secret Pentagon clearance for your visit to Cape Canaveral."

Bruce was stunned, "What visit?"

"The visit that President Kennedy ordered," responded Housman.

"No one told me," replied an excited and surprised Bruce.

"Roger that. That's what we're doing now. It's our job to see that the visit goes smoothly for you and one traveling partner of your choice," Major Housman explained.

"Well, when is it?" asked Bruce.

"We can't tell you that information because of its top secret nature. We don't just let anybody join events like this. All that we can tell you is to keep a bag packed and be ready to leave on a moment's notice," suggested the Major.

Bruce was beside himself and pleaded, "Don't you have any idea?"

"No," answered Captain Sparks.

"How will I know?" asked Bruce.

"Oh, don't worry. You will know. You must keep this conversation to yourself for now. We need your contact information along with some personal information including your home phone number, address, clothing and shoe sizes. In addition, we need a list of people to contact in case of an emergency," rattled off the Major.

Bruce's head was spinning. He felt as if he was in the middle of some spy thriller. He glanced at the two Air Force Officers and asked, "So this is really happening? This is no joke? The President kept his word? I'm really going to Cape Canaveral to see our first astronaut launched into space?"

Housman responded to Bruce's questions, "Given our orders, son, it looks as though the President kept his word."

Sparks added, "I don't know about the first launch, but I do know that you will see your share of astronauts. Your flight is going to be met by Colonel John 'Shorty' Powers at

Patrick Air Force Base when you arrive. He is the PIO for the whole astronaut program."

"I can hardly take it all in," thought Bruce and then he asked, "What's a PIO?"

"That's Public Information Officer, son," explained the Major. "He's just like me but a lot shorter. I'm the PIO for all of New York City."

Bruce was excited as he left the office and couldn't wait to tell his parents when he got home. Sitting around the dinner table that night he told his parents about the unexpected surprise meeting with the two Air Force Officers earlier in the day. They discussed who Bruce's traveling partner should be. In the end they all decided that Bruce should ask Mr. Kauffeld to join him.

Having made that decision Bruce's Mom helped him prepare and pack his bag before going to bed. He placed it in the hall closet by the front door so that he could leave at a moment's notice, just as he had been instructed.

When Bruce arrived at the office the next morning he went straight to Mr. Kauffeld's office and asked, "Is he in? I have something really important and amazing to ask him."

He was shown right in and immediately Bruce brought Mr. Kauffeld up to date. He shared his conversation with the Air Force officers and their instructions. He also told him about his family's discussion and decisions the night before. He asked, "Mr. Kauffeld, would you like to be my traveling partner and join me on the trip to the Cape? My family and I agree that you are the best choice."

Looking like a young kid opening a Christmas present, a surprised and very happy Ted Kauffeld said, "Bruce, I'm honored to join you. I will pack my bag too and wait for the call. This has turned into some adventure, hasn't it?"

"Yes, sir, it certainly has. Sometimes I don't even believe this is real. It's almost as if it's happening to someone else," responded Bruce honestly.

"Well, Bruce, I can say this. It's real and you're the one who started the ball rolling. I'm glad to be a part of all of it. Let's enjoy the ride, shall we?" said Mr. Kauffeld, smiling.

"Yes, sir, count me in!"

Bruce felt as though he was sitting on pins and needles every day wondering, "Will this be the day that the call comes? Is today the day?"

Several weeks passed without any calls. Before Bruce knew it February was gone and it was March. Time seemed to drift by as his anticipation continued to build.

It happened on a Saturday while he was doing chores out in the front yard for his Mom. He was wearing blue jeans, a T-shirt and a windbreaker. He was bent over, picking up some stuff that had blown into the yard and as he looked up he heard a car pull up to the curb. It was a black staff car with two Air Force guys in it. Running into the house he yelled to his Mom, "Mom, they're here!"

His Mom rushed around the corner and asked, "Who's here? What's going on."

"It's the Air Force guys, Mom!" replied Bruce.

She said, "Quick, run upstairs and change into your slacks. Get back down here as fast as you can and grab your bag out of the hall closet!"

Just then the doorbell rang and his Mom straightened her dress and hair and went to answer the door. She opened the door and saw two men in uniform standing on the porch waiting to talk to her. "Mrs. Tully?"

"Yes, I am," she answered.

"Can we see some ID, please? We have a release form for you to sign. We will be taking Bruce to the airport," he explained.

"Of course," she said.

Bruce made it back downstairs in record time. The release form was signed and returned to the officers.

They turned to Bruce and asked, "Do you have your clearance papers that Captain Sparks issued to you?"

"Yes, I do," Bruce replied.

The young airman looked them over and said, "Okay, they look good to me. Let's go."

His Mom watched as they turned and headed for the waiting car. Before getting into the car, Bruce turned and saw his Mom standing on the front porch. He waved "good-bye" and then ducked his head as he got into the car.

The drive to the airport was quiet. It wasn't long before they arrived at the Air Force Reserve hangar at Newark Airport. Captain Sparks met them as Bruce got out of the car just as another car pulled up and Mr. Kauffeld got out. They were all there and ready to go. Captain Sparks said, "It's good to see you again, Bruce," and turning around he said, "You must be Mr. Kauffeld. It is a pleasure to meet you, sir. It will be just a few minutes. Let me brief the pilot."

Once the briefing was completed Captain Sparks helped Bruce and Mr. Kauffeld board the Hercules C-130. He explained, "Our flight will take a little over three hours and we will land at Patrick Air Force Base in Coco Beach, Florida. Sit back, relax and enjoy your flight, gentlemen."

When they were in the air each one of them was given a box lunch that included a chilled deli sandwich, fruit and a candy bar. Bruce was impressed. The flight was uneventful and it gave him time to think about his parents and his family. He wondered what they were doing while he was on his way to Cape Canaveral. "This is unbelievable. I never would have guessed that I would be sitting here in the back of a C-130 flying to Cape Canaveral. How cool is this?"

Before long he heard Captain Sparks announce, "We're on our approach, so, buckle up. We will be landing in a few minutes."

CAPE CANAVERAL AND THE ASTRONAUTS

The landing was smooth and as Bruce stepped out of the plane and onto the tarmac he was greeted with warm Florida sunshine. "This is really different from the cold New Jersey weather we just left," he thought.

He immediately felt the hot sun on the back of his neck. It was his first trip to Florida and he didn't realize how hot it was. "Amazing! I just left cold and rain and now I can't wait to get out of my jacket."

Bruce saw a short, stocky, balding and commanding figure approach them as they walked across the tarmac. "Good afternoon, gentlemen. I'm Shorty Powers and I will be in charge of your stay for the next twelve days."

"Wow, they didn't tell me I was going to be here that long," Bruce thought.

Powers began to speak again and had to stop. It was hard to hear what he said because of a low-flying nearly supersonic flyby of an F-102 Delta Dart fighter interceptor. Bruce wondered, "That jet is no more than fifty feet off of the ground. How can it do that?"

They all watched the jet climb straight up, snap and roll into a 180-degree turn and then head for the end of the runway.

"Don't mind that. It's just Grissom and his way of saying welcome to the Cape! You will meet him later. I'm taking you to the Holiday Inn on the beach. This is where you will be quartered while you are here with us. It's also where all of us NASA types stay when we're working over at the Cape. I think you will enjoy it there," explained Shorty.

Shorty led them to the car and they all got in and headed to the Holiday Inn. It was a very short drive to the hotel and Powers helped them unload their bags. He said, "Once you're checked in, I will be back for both of you. We have a little reception planned out at the Cape. I will meet you in the lobby in thirty minutes."

Bruce and Mr. Kauffeld checked in easily and took their bags to their rooms. Then they met back in the lobby just as Shorty arrived—thirty minutes on the dot. "Let's head over to the Atlantic Coast Missile Firing Range," he said.

It was a short drive and they arrived quickly. As Shorty pulled his car into a large aircraft hangar Bruce saw several men milling around a table at the other end. "Who are those guys and what are they doing?" he wondered.

As they left the car the group of men noticed their arrival and slowly walked toward Bruce's group. Some of the men wore flight suits, others wore summer military uniforms and a few wore civilian clothes. As they came closer Bruce recognized all of them! "Wow, five of the Mercury Seven astronauts in the flesh. Man, I don't believe this."

Standing no more than three feet in front of Bruce and his group was a receiving line made up of Gordon "Gordo" Cooper, Jr., United States Air Force; John H. Glenn, Jr., United States Marine Corps; Virgil "Gus" Grissom, United States Air Force; Alan B. Shepard, Jr., United States Navy, and Donald "Deke" Slayton, United States Air Force. Scott Carpenter, United States Navy, and Walter "Wally" Schirra, United States Navy, weren't there because they were on assignment off base at another location. "This is unreal and beyond my wildest dreams," thought Bruce.

Shorty Powers was the first to speak. "This is the young man I told you about. He's here on orders from the President of the United States. He's being recognized for a significant and major accomplishment. His name is Bruce Tully and he's accompanied by his sponsor, Mr. Ted Kauffeld. Bruce will be here for the next two weeks and it's our job to see to it that he sees and experiences everything first-hand, everything that we're attempting to accomplish in the Mercury Seven program."

Bruce and Ted greeted each man in the informal receiving line. They shook each astronaut's hand. Bruce stopped and paused in front of each one and said, "It's truly my honor, sir, to meet you."

When he stepped in front of Alan B. Shepard, Jr. something unexpected happened. Bruce spoke first, "It's an honor to meet you, Commander Shepard."

Then to his surprise Shepard replied in a clear and strong voice, "No, you've got that wrong, Bruce. It's my honor to meet you. I saw you with Dave Garroway on the *Today Show* and I thought, 'I'm sure happy we have kids out there like this kid.' It's extraordinary what you're doing. I know I speak for all of us when I tell you that I'm sure glad the President sent you down here so we can thank you in person."

Bruce was speechless and taken off guard. He paused for a moment to collect his thoughts, then he shook Shepard's hand firmly and said, "Thank you, Commander Shepard, thank you so much."

What Bruce experienced during the following two weeks was beyond his wildest dreams. Each day he was assigned a mission specialist who gave him a complete tour and explanation of the mission section of the Cape that was that specialist's specialty. He sat in the Mercury capsule simulator and he toured launch block houses, missile gantries with live missiles preparing for launch, payload assembly areas, space suit fitting rooms and more.

This was a very special time for Bruce. He met and received briefings from some of the country's top scientists like Wernher von Braun. One of the most impressive parts of the trip for Bruce, besides meeting the astronauts, was observing missile launches. He watched the launches from inside block houses and at a very close range. He saw every size and shape of missile. They ranged from smaller high-speed, darting, solid-fueled missiles to the large payload, lumbering, liquid-fueled giants.

Another highlight of the trip for Bruce included the opportunity to observe a night launch of an Atlas D intercontinental ballistic missile. He was about a mile away from the launch site as he watched. He could hear the countdown and see searchlights shining on the rocket against a pitch black sky. As the engines burst into a torrent of flames a huge burst of light appeared to be someone turning on the sun! It lit up the whole area and the sky for miles in every direction. He watched the whole landscape change from night to looking like bright daylight in a matter of seconds.

Then it was like a shock wave hit him and he heard the loud, roaring engines and felt their power beating on his chest. He couldn't hear anything the noise was so loud. He felt the ground shake like an earthquake because of so much power from the launch. His insides felt as if they had turned to jelly. Everything was shaking and moving and his whole body felt as though it was vibrating. Then he saw the rocket begin to leave the ground slowly picking up speed fast and roaring like a dragon. He could see the light fade the higher it went. "Wow, that was extraordinary and amazing. I've never felt nor have I seen power like that."

Then he realized all of a sudden, "One of these astronauts will be sitting on top of that thing. I don't know if I would want to be the guy!"

Every day was packed with interesting things to do and filled with surprises. He spent time with each of the Mercury astronauts. He enjoyed the individual time spent in their work environments while they explained different aspects of the Mercury program and their mission assignments for the day.

So much was going on that Bruce felt as though his head was constantly spinning. He absorbed everything like a sponge taking everything in, but still wanting to experience more. "I'm the luckiest guy in the world," he thought.

As his two weeks came to an end at Cape Canaveral Bruce knew not an inch had been left unexplored. The trip finale included dinner with the astronauts and their wives who supported their husbands at the Cape. At dinner he was presented with a gold lapel pin of a miniature Mercury capsule and named an official Mercury program member.

Every aspect of the trip was perfect as far as Bruce was concerned, except for one thing. During his visit the United States was unsuccessful in launching the first man into space.

A number of reasons caused this, Alan Shepard told Bruce. Before leaving Shepard said, "Don't worry. Now that you're wearing the pin and you're one of us, kid, we're going to get you back down here when the time comes. That's a promise."

This helped ease Bruce's disappointment. Bruce and Mr. Kauffeld returned to New Jersey on March 30, 1961, with stories and very special memories to last them a lifetime.

MOMENTUM BUILDS

Once they returned it was back to work and their normal routine. Meetings accelerated with government officials. For the next two weeks the Astronarium team engaged in what came to be known as shuttle diplomacy making several trips back and forth to Washington, D.C.

They continued to build and gather support among a leading group of congressmen and senators while Bruce's Dad crossed the country enlisting support and endorsements from many notable educators and leading scientists. This included the well-known luminary, Dr. Edward Teller, who some believed to be the greatest mind on earth since Albert Einstein died in 1955.

Everything seemed to gain momentum and everything was going well until disaster struck on April 12, 1961. Nikita Khrushchev boldly announced to the world that the Soviet Union was the first nation to put a man into space. A young Russian Cosmonaut named Yuri Gagarin made history.

Bruce felt as though he had been kicked by a mule. "He will be in the history books like Columbus, Magellan and other adventurers," he thought. "It's going to be a Russian name and not an American name!"

"Time to regroup," he reasoned. "We need this project now more than ever. We have to help our kids!"

Despite what seemed like devastating news to Bruce he strengthened his resolve to dedicate himself to move his mission forward at all costs.

Within days of hearing the news he was contacted by the USAF PIO office in New York. "Mr. Tully, we want you to prepare yourself for an extended trip to the Cape, if you are interested," he heard.

"Of course I'm interested. I will be ready right away," Bruce responded.

MAKING HISTORY

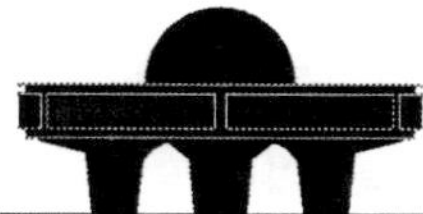

It felt like déjà vu. Once again he was picked up at home and taken to the airport where he boarded the flight for Patrick Air Force Base with Mr. Kauffeld. A car was waiting when they landed and, like before, they were delivered to the Coco Beach Holiday Inn.

This trip seemed very different once they arrived, however. It looked as if every press corps member was in town. Everywhere Bruce turned he bumped into one famous journalist after another. The Holiday Inn was full of famous people. He saw Walter Cronkite, Jules Bergman, Martin Cannon and Frank McGee. His media mentor, Dick Slawsky was there too.

When Bruce saw Dick he joined him and asked, "What's going on?"

Slawsky responded, "Given what just happened with the Soviets last week, we're all betting on a launch coming soon. We're ready to put the first American into space. The fact that you and Kauffeld were hustled down here verified it for me. They are going to light "the big candle" under one of our guys soon. We just don't know who or when."

"I had no idea. Will you stay close this week, Dick?" Bruce asked.

"Okay. Yeah, sure, kid. I will be keeping my eye on you from a distance. You can count on it. Hey, stay out of trouble and remember, no hustling the women down here or I will tell your Mom. She's a friend of mine, you know." teased Dick.

"Roger that, Dick," chuckled Bruce.

Bruce was aware that this trip was very different from the first one. "This trip is all about the Mercury Seven Manned Space Flight effort and the Mercury Seven astronauts. This is a lot more specific," he thought.

He was issued two passes by Colonel Powers. One pass gave him escorted access to classified work areas at the facility and the other, a press pass, gave Bruce access into a number of high level press briefings. "This is amazing. These briefings are reserved only for major members of the press corps," thought Bruce. "Man, this is too cool. Why me? I never expected this."

An earlier announcement had been made about the astronauts. Of the seven only three were candidates to go into space. Initially they were John Glenn, United States Marine Corps, oldest of the seven; Gus Grissom, United States Air Force; and Alan Shepard, United States Navy. All branches of the military were fairly represented during this prestigious event. Al Shepard joked that he definitely should be picked because when the capsule "splashed down," as a Naval Officer and graduate of the United States Naval Academy, he was the only one qualified to sail a boat!

From April 17, 1961, to the second day of May Bruce seemed to be attached to the hip of one astronaut or another as they went through their daily routines and training schedules. He accompanied each astronaut to the Cape and became each one's sidekick. He felt like a quiet "fly on the wall" while he observed the training rituals. Each day ended around 3:00 p.m. when everyone returned to the Holiday Inn to relax and hit the pool. Bruce was always invited to join the group and was considered to be "inside the ropes."

It was an honor to be included and to be able to "hang out" with these amazing astronauts. He joined in many lively chalk-talk sessions and was teased by them, just like one of them. He was the envy of the press corps. They didn't understand why Bruce had access to the astronauts and they didn't.

Some of the foreign press corps thought Bruce was a young "back up" astronaut in training, a role that he enjoyed playing. New York City reporters who knew him remained puzzled. To all of the others he was a mystery.

Bruce was approached by several reporters and they asked, "Hey, kid, who are you? Why are you here?"

One of the reporters who approached Bruce was James Elliott, Chief Military Editor from the *Norfolk Ledger Star*. After learning about him and his story he wrote a full-page article on May 18, 1961.

It was Monday, May 1, 1961. The astronauts and Bruce were having dinner at the Holiday Inn. The conversation focused on the Soviet May Day celebrations which highlighted their lead in the space race, well ahead of America's. No one at the table, including Bruce, was impressed.

After dinner Alan Shepard, who had taken Bruce under his wing, said, "Hey, Bruce, how about having some apple pie and ice cream up in my room? I have a pretty neat gadget up there I want to show you."

Bruce didn't have to be asked twice. "You bet, Commander Shepard. Count me in!"

He thought, "Pie and ice cream and a one-on-one with Commander Shepard. I can't turn this down."

Bruce and Commander Shepard went upstairs. Bruce was amazed. NASA had installed a total mock-up simulator of the Mercury capsule control panel in the Commander's room. "This is what he wanted to show me," thought Bruce.

Just as the Commander started explaining the control panel the phone rang. "I had better take this call, Bruce."

Shepard became very serious as he listened to the caller. He didn't have much to say. He listened intently. About halfway through the call Bruce realized the President of the United States must be on the other end of the line. He remained very quiet.

He heard Shepard say, "Yes, sir. Yes, sir."

Then he asked, "So, then she can be at the launch site? Yes, sir, Mr. President, thank you very much. This means a lot to me."

It was a call from President Kennedy. "If I was a reporter, this would be the hottest news scoop of the year," Bruce thought.

Bruce began to put the pieces together as Shepard hung up the phone and turned around. He pointed his finger at Bruce and spoke directly, "You never heard this call. Do you understand me?"

Bruce knew Shepard was all business and quickly responded, "What call? I didn't hear any call. What are you talking about?"

Shepard knew that Bruce wouldn't betray his trust. This call was the one that confirmed Commander Alan B. Shepard, Jr., United States Navy, would be the first American into space, carrying the nation's hopes and dreams with him. His wife, Louise, would be present in the block house at launch time. Bruce and Shepard took a few more minutes with the simulator but cut their visit short after the President's call.

He left Commander Shepard and returned to the pool area where he listened to conversations from the press corps who speculated about which astronaut would be the first into space. Large sums of money were placed on the table and from what he overheard it seemed that most of the press thought Shepard was a long shot. The conventional favorite was John Glenn, given his age and status.

Bruce observed and smiled to himself. He knew who it was but kept his mouth shut. "There's no way I'm going to break my promise to the Commander," Bruce vowed.

He overheard Marty Cannon bet five hundred dollars on Glenn just then. Bruce thought, "If I were a betting man and had the money, I could earn enough to put myself through college just by being here tonight."

Quickly he banished that thought from his head. He knew he wouldn't betray the Commander's confidence and went back to drinking his coke. He didn't stay too much longer. Quickly he headed back to his room for some sleep.

All week everyone felt as if they were killing time. They knew a launch would happen. You could feel the excitement in the air. All of the details were Top Secret because of a fear that the launch would be sabotaged. With the Cold War tensions and the Russians' launching first a lot of people were feeling paranoid. Bruce noticed that shortly after his meeting with Shepard in his room they moved Shepard, Glenn, and Grissom from the Holiday Inn to Cape Canaveral.

IT'S A GO!

It was May 5, 1961, and Bruce heard a knock on the door at 3:00 a.m. He was escorted to the Redstone rocket missile control block house. Although it was early the morning was crisp, brisk and clear. He saw the rocket with the Mercury capsule on top of it. It was bathed in powerful light with floodlights shining from every direction.

Many of the launch officials were already there. Everyone was focused intensely on the tasks at hand. Bruce knew some of the specialists and enjoyed seeing them in action on such an important occasion. This was the real deal and not a drill.

The countdown began and the launch was a "go!" In a matter of a few short hours Commander Alan B. Shepard, Jr., would make history. He was the first American astronaut to be launched into space. This was a momentous occasion. He was the only one that would be inside the Mercury capsule that he named *Freedom Seven*.

Upon launch he would travel one hundred sixteen miles to the edge of space at a terminal velocity of over 5,100 miles per hour. Splashdown was targeted for three hundred two miles downrange in the Atlantic Ocean. It was a suborbital ballistic shot but it breached the barriers of space just the same.

Bruce was outside when Shepard arrived at the gantry tower for his ride up to the capsule. He got out of the transport van looking very confident. He looked around quickly at the people who were there, waved and stepped into the elevator.

"That's no stranger," thought Bruce. "He's my friend and teacher. He made time for me this week, the most important week of my life. He thought I was important even though he's the one making history. He's the first American to go into space."

Bruce was honored and proud to be at this historical launch. "I get to witness history being made. This is the stuff that dreams are made of. I never imagined when I conceived the idea for the Astronarium and Science Center two years ago after Khrushchev's challenge that I would be here! I never dreamed I would be involved in something like this. I only wanted to help America's kids and make a difference when I accepted the challenge. I didn't have any clue how I could make my vision happen.

In the middle of all of the intense activity he continued to think: "It's taken a lot of hard work and perseverance. I'm living my mission. My vision is real. So many people have helped me. It's all been worth it. It's brought me here. I want to remember this moment forever."

Bruce looked up and realized that Shepard was safe in the capsule. It was time for him to move to the forward observation area with his escort where he could watch the launch with the members of the press. Looking around he saw every famous journalist and news anchor in the area. Each one of them wanted to get the best viewing position, a place where they could see and report on the launch. Bruce looked around for Dick Slawsky and walked over to him. "Have they been keeping you busy?" Slawsky asked.

"Yeah, I just saw Shepard go up to the capsule before I came over here," replied Bruce.

"Shepard is in for some ride when they light that firecracker today," proclaimed Slawsky. "He's going to be hanging on for dear life. Man, what a ride!"

Bruce snapped back, "Yeah, he's got the courage to do it."

"Yeah," responded Slawsky. "These test pilot types are a breed apart. They are not like you and me."

Precisely at 9:34 a.m., Friday, May 5, 1961, on top of a Redstone rocket, Shepard rode into the history books. Bruce was there to see that history being made. "I was supposed to be some stupid kid from New Jersey that nobody would listen to, according to my Dad. I am thankful. I've sure come a long way!"

Shortly after the launch it was time for Bruce and Mr. Kauffeld to return home and to go back to work.

A CONGRESSIONAL COMMITTEE INVITATION

Bruce had been back a week when he was contacted by staff members from the New York City office of Congressman Victor Anfuso. Victor Anfuso was the Chairman of the House Science and Astronautic Committee. He was aware of Bruce's efforts to build the Astronarium and Science Center and had met Bruce at the White House. The Congressman was in the process of sponsoring a bill to create an additional service academy. Instead of a military academy it would be an academy dedicated to create the best scientists and engineers in the country.

Bruce was asked to share his vision with the Committee. On Thursday, May 25, 1961, with his father and mother at his side, Bruce agreed to appear before the Committee. He was the youngest U.S. Citizen to testify before a Congressional Committee in both the House of Representatives and the Senate of the United States.

As Bruce spoke the audience was mesmerized. They were impressed with the wisdom and intelligence that this young man shared during the hearing. He finished his presentation by challenging the Committee, "If I can take up this cause alone as a sixteen-year-old kid, then you guys as Congressmen can get it done."

His testimony was a huge success and he was congratulated at length by each Committee member. That very afternoon he learned that earlier that day President Kennedy issued his own challenge in a speech that committed the United States of America to land a man on the moon by the end of the decade. "The Soviets may have won the race to orbit the earth, but we are going to win the race to the moon," he thought.

Bruce breathed a sigh of relief and thought, "Someone else has finally joined me in my personal battle with Khrushchev. Who better than the President of the United States?"

A SURPRISING AND UNEXPECTED INVITATION

When he got home that evening he noticed that a personal copy of *Progressive Architecture* was waiting for him on the kitchen table, the same table where he drew his first set of drawings for the Astronarium and Science Center. As he thumbed through the magazine, looking at the latest nationally recognized architectural designs, he saw it! In the May 1961 issue he saw a full-page article about the Astronarium and Science Center. He was excited and amazed. "It happened! Wes Weidner will be proud. We made it into *Progressive Architecture*. This was one of our goals!"

After giving his testimony to the Congressional Committee Bruce received an unbelievable letter. It was an engraved invitation that carried the hammer and sickle of the Soviet Union. Bruce and his Mom were shocked to find something from the USSR in their mailbox so he called his friend Major Housman for his advice. He described the invitation and the Major thought for a few minutes and then said, "Go ahead and open it, Bruce."

"Major Housman, this is unbelievable. It's an invitation from the Union of Soviet Socialist Republics (USSR), Ministry of Education and Science," said a shaky Bruce as he read what was inside.

He looked at his Mom in total disbelief as he continued to read the document to Major Housman. "It's an invitation to me as an expatriated son of Russia to return to the Soviet Union as an honored guest of the USSR. I'm invited to attend the next Leipzig Science Fair that is going to be held in East Germany. They want to honor me for the work I've done on the Astronarium and Science Center. I can't believe it. How do they know about my work?"

The next day, with the help of Dick Slawsky, Bruce got in touch with officials at the State Department. They quickly let him know that under no circumstances would the United States allow him to attend the Soviet-sponsored event. They offered to decline the Soviet's invitation politely on his behalf. They believed the Soviet Union would try to make some strange attempt to claim Bruce, given his Russian heritage. Then they would find a way to create propaganda if Bruce accepted the invitation.

The State Department told Bruce that he was a symbol of true American youth. He wasn't what Khrushchev had attempted to characterize as American youth during his rant at the United Nations. Bruce saw this action as a crushing blow to deliver to Khrushchev.

It was clear the Soviets knew who Bruce was. He felt good about rejecting their offer. "I'm satisfied that I've accomplished a big part of the mission I created almost twenty-two months ago."

YOUTH ARE OUR FUTURE

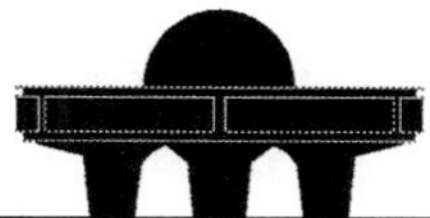

During his two visits to Cape Canaveral Bruce had become close friends with Captain Ferris Smith, a missile launch officer. Smith was an Annapolis graduate in engineering and understood and appreciated Bruce's mission. He shared the same viewpoint regarding America's youth and wanted to find ways to stimulate kids' interests in pursuing advanced engineering careers. Bruce encouraged Captain Smith to create a traveling lecture on the many activities taking place at Cape Canaveral including dramatic film of missile launches—successes and failures.

After receiving approval for a leave from his regular duties for a short time to tour New Jersey's high schools he joined Bruce to begin the lectures. Having spent almost six weeks at Cape Canaveral Bruce was more excited than ever. He wanted to share with his classmates and other students all of the wonders he had experienced with the astronauts while he was at the Cape. He thought this was a great way to share the story of the Astronarium and Science Center as well. Smith thought doing the presentations together with Bruce was a great idea and he arranged for his leave to begin the first week of June.

Prior to Captain Smith's arrival Bruce contacted each of the school principals and offered to come to their schools. He explained what would be presented. The principals were excited and agreed to arrange for school-wide assemblies so that the entire student body could see the presentations.

Madison High School, Bruce's former school, was one of the schools scheduled. He couldn't wait to return to the place where he was almost expelled for working on his project. It's funny how things change. Now his project opened doors to audiences and respect from congressmen, senators, astronauts, and the President of the United States.

In his own way Bruce was somewhat of a celebrity. As he thought about the upcoming presentations he wondered, "How will my former friends, classmates, teachers and school administrators receive me? This is the place where my journey began."

He was about to find out as he and Captain Smith arrived at the school. They were greeted by a receiving line that included Dr. Ward Shoemaker, Principal Rogers, Dean Garrala, and several of his former teachers. Dr. Shoemaker spoke first, "Welcome back, Bruce. We have all been following your progress with great interest. Let me be the first to congratulate you for your accomplishments."

Principal Rogers spoke next. "We're honored to have you make room for us on your lecture tour, Bruce, and we look forward to seeing what you and Captain Smith have in store for us today. Captain Smith, do you need any assistance with your audio-visual equipment?"

"Here's a list of what I need to have set up in the auditorium. Thank you for taking care of it," responded Captain Smith.

Two audio-visual students appeared and took the Captain's slide trays and reels of film to the auditorium to get things set up for the assembly. Then Bruce and the Captain were escorted to the teacher's private dining room for lunch. While they ate Bruce thought, "Man, a year ago I couldn't get anywhere close to this room and now, look! I've crashed the sacred inner sanctum of the teacher's private dining room."

Feeling very satisfied he sat and took it all in. Before he knew it lunch was over and it was time to leave for the assembly. As they left the dining room and walked down the halls many memories stirred for Bruce. He was in his own world reminiscing when they entered a large room that was noisy. He felt excitement from all of the kids that were there. He and Captain Smith slowly walked down the aisle and a hush fell over the student body. As he reached the front of the room all eyes turned and focused on him. You could hear a pin drop. As the room quieted he heard the voice of his old friend, Charlie Walker, in the back of the auditorium, "Tully, the man to get the job done!"

Immediately a deep rumbling chant followed from the jocks, "Bruce! Bruce! Bruce!"

The Dean of Men yelled, "Silence!"

The room quieted and order was restored. Everyone could see the boy who wore jeans and a varsity letter jacket was gone and in his place stood a confident young man in a Brooks Brothers' suit. It was an amazing transformation.

As the student body quieted Bruce stepped up to the microphone. His manner was friendly and inviting. He was poised and spoke with confidence and maturity as he explained the purpose of the presentation.

Then he introduced Captain Smith and turned the presentation over to him. For the next two hours the students were captivated and at certain points you could hear a lot of "oohs" and "ahs." When the lights came on and it was Bruce's turn to speak he said, "I hope that in some small way this presentation encourages some of you to consider a future in science and technology. Amazing opportunities are available and our country needs more people like this."

Looking at the audience he saw one of his old teammates slouching in his seat and wearing a varsity letterman's sweater. It was DeAngelo, the player that he had had the locker room confrontation with a year ago. He turned to him, "As for you milk haters that have never tasted milk, I seriously recommend that you TASTE IT. I did. Look what it's done for me!"

After a few more closing comments the presentation was over and the students broke into thunderous cheers and applause. The nerds rushed up to the front of the room so they could shake Bruce's hand. After congratulations were offered and accepted, Bruce and the Captain left through a rear exit. "This must be how a rock star feels," thought Bruce.

As he walked away and looked back over his shoulder he saw DeAngelo standing at one of the windows looking at him. "I feel like the prodigal son returning home. Man, I could have been that guy! All I want to do now is keep walking into the future!" thought Bruce.

AMAZING DECISIONS AND TRIPS

Amazing events continued to happen to Bruce as the round of presentations finished.

Five days later on June 10, 1961, he returned to Andrews Air Force Base in Washington, D.C., and received formal support for his project on behalf of the Air Force from Lieutenant General Bernard Shriever, Commander of the United States Air Force Systems Command.

On July 21, 1961, Bruce was informed by Congressman Victor Anfuso that the Astronarium and Science Center was not selected for the 1964 World's Fair. His concept, however, would be used as a model for the future development of a new Space and Astronautics Museum that Anfuso and other Congressmen were looking to appropriate funds to build.

After this announcement a disappointed Bruce took a year to travel and investigate the Western Coast of the United States. Then he returned to Madison, New Jersey, where he graduated from Madison High School in June of 1963.

In 1975 the new Space and Astronautics Museum was opened as part of the Smithsonian Museum on the Washington

Mall in Washington, D.C. Bruce's model played an important role in its design. Today it is one of the most attended museums in the United States.

After high school Bruce went on to college to earn degrees in architecture and urban planning, landscape architecture and regional analysis. He holds a PhD in Environmental Science. Today, Dr. Tully is the CEO of a national planning, engineering and environmental consulting firm.

VICTORIA'S EPILOGUE

As the story, *Act of One*, unfolded I kept asking myself, "What motivates a sixteen-year-old teenage jock, who grew up in the 1950s, to do what he did? Where did his vision come from? How did he keep going against all odds? How did he accomplish what he did and end up meeting the President of the United States, the Mercury Seven astronauts as well as other leaders in government and industry?

Pretty amazing, isn't it?

Many of you might say, "He was born this way," or, "It's part of his genetic make-up," while others might say, "He was lucky."

What makes one person move forward into the unknown while another person chooses to stay where they are and avoid risks?

My point in raising these questions isn't to decide what motivated Bruce. Rather, it's to ask, "Was Bruce's story really about designing the Astronarium and all that went with it? Or was it something more?

For me his story clearly speaks to something more. Through Bruce's vision, mission and actions in *Act of One* we journey with him through the many stages of his personal growth and transformation. We see him mature from a sixteen-year-old teenage jock and become a man. His experiences serve as a rite of passage and a way to solidify a firm foundation of values that will support him for the rest of his life. These are the same values he observed daily as a young boy spending time with his Grandpa Joseph and they included courage, vision, perseverance, integrity, faith and trust among others.

Bruce took advantage of the opportunities to expand and strengthen his visionary, leadership and speaking skills beginning on the football field and throughout his journey. These skills served him well as he was invited to speak before industry leaders, television audiences, a Congressional Committee as well as high school students and administrators. Later they continued to serve him as a successful business entrepreneur. He became a visionary who innovatively founded and sold four diverse companies as he grew professionally.

Act of One demonstrates that anyone, regardless of age, can make a difference. Not only did Bruce personally grow and gain from his experiences. He touched many lives and gained great support and help along the way for his Astronarium project from very influential people as he focused on accomplishing his mission.

He provided hope and inspired others by his example and demonstrated that young people can make a difference and be very responsible. Young people can see a bigger picture and they can problem-solve solutions that can have a major impact on community, government, society and the world, if we support them.

In many ways Bruce's efforts can be viewed as heroic. Today many of our kids' heroes are fantasy and science fiction characters. The field is clear for someone else like Bruce A. Tully who can identify a problem, see a vision and take action—someone who inspires others.

Bruce showed us that anything is possible when we persevere and gather the right people and resources together as we focus on a common goal. This type of leadership is needed now and is ageless. Although this true story takes place during the 1950s and 1960s, I believe the message is timeless. Now it is time for us to support the ageless innovators and visionaries who can help us solve our problems and we need to assist them on their journeys.

Science and technology advancement are still issues. Health, education, our environment, socio-economy and other areas of our lives leave room for great improvement. We have access to limitless possibilities that can help resolve these issues if we "let go" of perceived limitations, just as Bruce did, and if we don't give up.

"Hearing" one another with open minds and hearts will assist in finding answers to problems that may be viewed as "out of the box." It is essential to encourage creativity and action, to provide tools and resources as well as experiences and mentoring needed to support current and future visionaries, leaders and innovators.

BRUCE'S EPILOGUE

When we reflect back on the period during which this story occurred, one thing stands out to me: the state of mind of our nation. We were at the height of the Cold War tensions that existed between the Soviet Union and the United States of America. Many of our citizens truly doubted and questioned whether we as a country had the will and wherewithal to stand up to the ever-growing threat of Communism to our way of life.

With every day it appeared that we were slowly falling behind the accomplishments that were occurring in the Eastern Block. Many emerging Third World countries were turning to the notion that Socialism and Communism offered better ways of life to their citizens than our model of a free economy based on capitalism and democracy. They even had a term for it; they called it "the domino effect." Communism was growing worldwide—in Asia, Africa, Central America, and a few miles south of Florida, in Cuba! It seemed that our way of life was under attack from all directions.

We were a nation facing many problems; political, social and economic were but a few. An air of fear and apathy was slowly spreading throughout the land, while people waited for the next guy to come up with the answers to their problems.

The essence of the story in *Act of One* is the fact that a young boy of sixteen years did not wait around for someone, or something, or some government to solve what he perceived as a *matter of great national importance*. He chose to act as a force of one, alone and on his own. He took action and moved forward with the meager resources that he was able to muster on his own. He did not falter in the face of huge obstacles or quit just because things got tough. He persevered and kept moving forward until he accomplished his mission. He accomplished all of this without computers, the Internet, a cell phone, Facebook or Google. Impossible, right?

Then why has it taken over fifty years to have this story told? Some say every story has its time and it is in this time, the second decade of a new millennium, that the events in the story of an *Act of One* need to be told.

We, once more, find our nation to be a nation in a state of crisis. We have withstood terrorism and attacks on our homeland for the first time in our nation's history. We continue to be at war in the Middle East and many in the world wish to see our way of life destroyed. In addition, we have suffered and continue to suffer through a great economic recession that has shaken our basic beliefs in our country and its economic system. Many have lost faith in our political leaders and the system in which they function.

Because of these events never has it been a better time to tell the story of *Act of One* than today. The essence of this story is timeless and it applies now as well as it did over fifty years ago when I was moved to a call for action out of love for my country, its people and our way of life.

It is my sincere hope that if by reading *Act of One* the story moves just one individual to act with a sense of total commitment and perseverance to solving any one of the matters of great national importance that face our country today, then my actions of over fifty years ago will have been more than worth the effort.

The time for waiting for the next guy to solve our problems is over.

Become an *Act of One*!

INTRODUCTION TO APPENDIX I – ROBERT YOWELL

July 2012

The path that lead me to discover the story of Dr. Tully's amazing achievements as a high school student in New Jersey in 1961 would not have been possible without the advent of the Internet. That being said, it is remarkable today to consider that Bruce was able to achieve what he did, and even have the ear of the Congress and President of the United States, without the use of a computer or cellular phone.

We take for granted today the ease with which we can find information instantly, create wonderful Powerpoint slides, and reach people's email accounts.

What Dr. Bruce Tully's story teaches us is that hard work and dedication are timeless attributes achieved using only one's mind and soul as the tools.

INTRODUCTION TO APPENDIX I – ROBERT YOWELL 261

As you read in the preceding pages, Bruce's talents were eventually recognized and encouraged by those around him who believed in his goals. Bruce has given us great principles for the road to success: believe in yourself, persevere, and surround yourself with those who believe in you.

(From August 2000 through February 2009 Robert Yowell held various positions at Aerospace Corporation. He was Senior Mission Manager of SpaceX for a year until February 2010. From October 2010 until April 2011 Robert Yowell served as Senior Analyst for Cobham Analytic Solutions. From April 2011 to the present he has been Chief Engineer, Evolved Expendable Launch Vehicle, United States Air Force.)

APPENDIX I

Background: Theodore Kauffeld's
professional rendering of the Astronarium.
Foreground: Kauffeld and Bruce Tully discuss a
model that Tully built in his high school shop class.
Air and Space Smithsonian, September 2011.

Drawing: copyright and courtesy of Robert Yowell.

Photo: Library of Congress.

ABOVE AND BEYOND: TULLY'S ASTRONARIUM
A high-schooler champions science in America.
by Robert Yowell

In 2006, I purchased on eBay a set of original architectural drawings of a building called an Astronarium, dated January 1961. It was inscribed on the front page "Best Regards to Bruce, From the Mercury Astronauts." I bought the set because it combined two of my passions: spaceflight (I have been an engineer in the U.S. space program for the last 20 years) and the 1964–65 New York World's Fair. It appeared to have been a proposal for a large space-themed exhibit for the fair, featuring a large planetarium dome surrounded by exhibits and lecture rooms. The drawings were signed by five of the seven astronauts; only Wally Schirra and Scott Carpenter were missing. The eBay seller had no idea who Bruce was. All he knew was that the set of drawings was purchased from the estate of a butler who lived in a New Jersey mansion.

Who was Bruce, and why did the Mercury astronauts sign his drawings?

An Internet search on "astronarium" pulled up only a few hits; the most useful, a newspaper archive with a 1961 article about a high school senior, Bruce Tully, who had come up with the idea. Now I had a full name. But that alone was not enough, so my search was relegated to the back burner.

Five years later I did another Internet search on "astronarium." Up came the University of Texas library, which had obtained the photo morgue of the long-defunct *New York*

Journal American newspaper. There was one photograph listed of an "Astronarium proposed for New York World's Fair." The library had scanned the photo, which depicted one of the drawings from the set that I had; on the back, a caption named the designer, Bruce A. Tully. A search on the full name found Dr. Bruce A. Tully's biography on the Web site for his company, the Trapezium Consulting Group. I e-mailed him, and he promptly replied: Yes, he was the same Bruce Tully, now 67. For the past 40 years, he had worked in environmental consulting, urban planning, and civil engineering. And, he told me, there was so much more to the Astronarium story.

In 1959, 15-year-old Bruce A. Tully of Madison, New Jersey High School sat in the viewing gallery of the United Nations General Assembly with his civics class, listening through his earpiece to an interpreter as Soviet Premier Nikita Khrushchev chastised the United States for its imperialism and the underachievement of its youth. Tully was driven to showcase American ingenuity and engineering expertise. In a few years, New York would be hosting a World's Fair; Tully envisioned as the fair's centerpiece an Astronarium, comprising a planetarium and exhibits on astronautics and space travel. He wrote a thesis on the Astronarium and built a scale model in his shop class.

In the summer of 1960, Tully took his model to the head of every large corporation in Manhattan. At Shell Oil, he noticed that the president took a private elevator to his office, bypassing the lobby. Tully, model in hand, confronted the executive at the elevator and explained the rationale behind the Astronarium.

The Shell man offered to call Theodore J. Kauffeld, whose civil engineering firm, Devenco, designed chemical refineries for Shell. Tully was whisked in a limousine to 150 Broadway, where Kauffeld offered the services of his engineers and architects.

Since much of Tully's time was spent in Manhattan, his parents enrolled him in Rhodes Preparatory School, designed for child actors and other young professionals (alumni include James Caan and Robert DeNiro). For a year, Tully spent afternoons working at Devenco, where he was paid $65 a week. The company produced a set of drawings and an architectural model of an Astronarium, which would tower 345 feet and house a planetarium projector from the firm Carl Zeiss.

Tully's project caught the attention of the science editor for the *New York World-Telegram and Sun*, who wrote a series on the Astronarium's progress, which was read by U.S. Congressman Victor Anfuso of New York, a member of the House Committee on Science and Astronautics. In January 1961, Anfuso introduced a bill, H.R. 1, calling for the establishment of a National Science Academy to "help meet our pressing national problems in science and engineering education." Anfuso endorsed Tully's Astronarium, which could serve as a showcase at the World's Fair and remain as a permanent home of the academy. Anfuso arranged a meeting in Washington with the Secretary of

Commerce and the presidential committee tasked to plan the U.S. government's presence at the fair. On January 16, Tully appeared on NBC's *Today* show with host Dave Garroway, drawing national attention to the Astronarium.

Tully's Washington visit occurred in the first weeks of President John F. Kennedy's administration. Tully, his parents, and Theodore Kauffeld were invited to lunch at the White House. Kennedy joined Tully at the table for a hamburger, told him he was a credit to the nation, and asked, "What would you like me to do?"

"How about a trip to the Cape to see our first man launch in space?"

"I can do that," Kennedy replied.

On a Saturday morning in March, while Tully was cutting the grass, a military staff car pulled into the driveway to take him to the Newark Airport. A military transport flew him to Patrick Air Force Base, Florida, at Cape Canaveral, where John "Shorty" Powers, a NASA public affairs officer who became known as "the voice of Mercury Control," was waiting for him. At Hangar S, the seven Mercury astronauts were lined up to greet him. To Alan Shepard, the last in line, Tully said, "Mr. Shepard, it is an honor to meet you," to which Shepard replied, "No, Bruce, it is an honor to meet you. I watched you on the *Today Show* and was very impressed."

Tully accompanied the Mercury Seven on scuba trips and simulations, and stayed with them at the Holiday Inn in Cocoa Beach. There he deduced which of the final three—Gus

Grissom, John Glenn, and Alan Shepard—would be the first American in space: He saw a Mercury capsule instrument panel simulator in Shepard's hotel room.

One day, while he was in Shepard's room for ice cream and pie, the phone rang and Tully heard Shepard say, "Yes sir, thank you for allowing her to do this. Thank you, Mr. President." To Tully he said, "You never heard that phone call." Kennedy had told Shepard that Shepard's wife, Louise, would be in the blockhouse during the *Freedom 7* launch, where Shepard would say his final goodbye to her from the capsule. (Due to postponements, Louise was not in the blockhouse on launch day.)

On May 5, 1961, Tully awoke before sunrise and watched Shepard enter the astronaut transit van, which took off for the Mercury-Redstone launch site. He then watched the launch from the press area.

Three weeks later, on May 25, Kennedy announced the nation's goal of landing a man on the moon and returning him to Earth "before this decade is out." Earlier that afternoon, 17-year-old Bruce Tully testified on Capitol Hill in support of Anfuso's National Science Academy bill, armed with letters of support from Edward Teller, Gerard Kuiper, and Donald Douglas.

In the end, the United States chose a different theme structure for the World's Fair, and despite Anfuso's efforts, the National Science Academy facility was never constructed.

So why were the Astronarium drawings in a New Jersey mansion for almost 50 years? That was Kauffeld's house. Tully says he and Kauffeld brought the drawings to Cape Canaveral during the 1961 visit, where the astronauts signed them. He recalls seeing Scott Carpenter and Wally Schirra only briefly, which explains why their signatures are missing. Kauffeld never gave the signed set to Tully, leaving it as a mystery for me to solve, and then relay the whole story 50 years later.

APPENDIX I 269

INTRODUCTION TO APPENDIX II – VICTORIA

We are pleased to share these personal photos and articles that survived a basement flood several years ago.

Here are photos of Bruce A. Tully, Theodore J. Kauffeld, a third-rendition design and an artist's rendering of the Astronarium and Science Center as well as three newspaper articles describing his project.

INTRODUCTION TO APPENDIX II 271

APPENDIX II

Bruce A. Tully – Originator of the Project

A transformed Bruce wearing his Brooks Brothers' suit
and Mercury Seven lapel pin!

Theodore J. Kauffeld – Sponsor of the Project

Without Mr. Kauffeld's help Bruce Tully's
finished project wouldn't exist.
He believed in Bruce and his vision.

Astronarium and Science Center

The refined, third-rendition design by LaPierre,
Litchfield & Partners Associate Architects. First was
Bruce's original model. The second rendition was
created during Bruce's summer program. This
refined rendition is a joint collaboration
between Bruce and the architects.

Proposed Astronarium and Science Center for the 1964
New York World's Fair – 9 January 1961

An artist's rendering set in context of the World's
Fair which shows scale and relationship to pedestrians.

Photo by Ravens.

Bruce Tully (right) explains the planetarium and science center he is proposing for the World's Fair to Theodore J. Kauffeld, the consulting engineer who is so impressed with young Tully's ideas that he has put him on his payroll.

Genius, 17, to Give Fair His 'Astronarium' Plan

By ALEX BENSON,
World-Telegram Staff Writer.

An international engineering firm hopes to present the World's Fair Corp. and the federal government completed blueprints for a mammoth science center and planetarium drawn by a 17-year-old New Jersey youth, it was learned today.

The young designer is Bruce Tully of Westfield. A student at the Rhodes School mornings, Bruce has worked for months in the afternoon as a paid employee of Theodore J. Kauffeld, consulting engineer, 150 Broadway.

The tall, gangling youth is "a genius," asserts Mr. Kauffeld. His general plans for a spectacular "astronarium" were finished weeks ago.

Announcement Discouraging.

An artist was at work on a pictorial presentation when the Fair Corp. announced last Monday it was recommending a similar idea to be the United States exhibit at the 1964-65 exposition.

Although Bruce says he is "discouraged and disappointed" at the Fair Corp. announcement because it might mean the Fair was committed to someone else's proposal, Mr. Kauffeld said he plans to go right ahead and contact the Fair Corp. anyway, as well as the federal government.

"I think Bruce's idea is the best anyone has come up with and merits consideration," Mr. Kauffeld said. "We have already invested $50,000 developing this and it is advanced far beyond any other proposal."

Article Spotted.

The engineer told of reading about Bruce's idea in a newspaper article last June. "I thought it was a fantastically good idea."

"I took him on my staff at $85 a week, put my personnel and facilities at his disposal and told him to draw up the plans."

Bruce's drawings show a domed circular structure housing on the top floor the largest planetarium in the world—100 feet in diameter. There is also a lobby engineered for one-way traffic flow and a ring-like exhibition floor rimming the dome as well as other space.

Bruce said he got the idea for his project after a couple of visits to the Hayden Planetarium two years ago. He said he thought the Hayden Planetarium was "obsolete" in design.

Bruce is the son of Mr. and Mrs. Anthony Tully. Mr. Tully is an independent television producer.

New York World-Telegram and Sun,
Friday, December 1960

YOUNG DESIGNER AT CAPE CANAVERAL—Bruce Tully of Westfield (right), designer of an astronarium-science center which he hopes will become a national science building, and Theodore J. Kauffield, New York consulting engineer, who is backing the project, are briefed in Cape Canaveral, Fla., by Capt. Ferris Smith, USAF, on the Titan Missile Project of which the platforms in the background are a part. (Official Air Force Photo)

Young Scientist Visits Astronauts

Plainfield Currier News, March 30, 1961

High School Senior Spurs $33 Million Space Sc[ience]

By WARD CANNEL

CONVENT, N. J. (NEA).— This story is about a high school senior named Bruce Tully and why it has fallen on his shoulders to direct a $33 million space science project, when there are so many experts around nowadays.

"All of a sudden," young Bruce recalls, "I got fed up with what I was hearing all around me about the space age.

"The kids were saying they didn't want careers in science because it was too complicated to understand. And the adults were saying they didn't want to hear any more about space because you couldn't understand it even when it was explained.

"Well, I'm no space expert. But I could see what was wrong. The experts weren't telling the story of our achievements and goals and purpose correctly."

SO, ONE NIGHT Bruce sat down with a ruler and a mixing bowl and paper and pencils and designed an answer to the problem.

It was a new kind of machine, housed in a new kind of building — an invention that has since been called an Astronarium. According to Bruce's plans, it was a university holding everything necessary for the understanding of our new age.

There were lecture rooms, exhibit halls, library facilities, TV—everything. And in the center, a huge new kind of planetarium using 3-D and stereo to make the story of space conquest real and, more important, understandable to kids and adults.

"IT LOOKED pretty good," Bruce said, "so I rolled the plans up and went out to find somebody to build it." I talked to bankers and architects and contractors, and finally somebody told me about a very important consulting engineer named T. J. Kauffeld who lived about a mile from our house."

It was a Sunday night, Kauffeld recalls. The butler came into the dining room and said a young boy was at the door.

BRUCE TULLY (left) and T. J. KAUFFELD
. . . with schoolboy's model of Astronarium

"I figured it was collection for the Boy Scouts," Kauffeld said. "I had the boy wait in the library. After dinner I went in to see him and the first words he hit me with were: 'Mr. Kauffeld, what are you doing for the future scientists of America?' "

KAUFFELD LOOKED at young Bruce's plans. They were almost perfect in every detail—capacity, dimension, conception.

"I forgot that he was a high school junior," Kauffeld said. "I knew I was talking with a genius. I told him to come to my New York office the next morning."

Kauffeld put Bruce on the payroll at $65 per week, gave him an unlimited expense account and turned over a staff of engineers and draftsmen to him.

That was a year ago.

SINCE THEN, while Kauffeld had been conferring with legislators and investors, Bruce has been working out the bugs in the exhibits with U. S. space experts at Cape Canaveral, designing the 3-D projector with a German optical company and finishing the building plans with the architects.

Kauffeld estimates that $100,000 has already been spent on the Astronarium. The building itself will cost about $33 million—"an average job for my company.

"And if the New York World's Fair doesn't take it or the government doesn't want it, we'll put it up ourselves. It'll cost about $1 million in gate receipts."

Space Science Project
Begins to Take Shape

Teenager's $33 Million Idea

The Amazing Story of Bruce Tully, New Jersey High School Senior

—— Page 6 ——

Philadelphia Daily News, Monday, April 17, 1961